How to Master
the Art of Selling
FINANCIAL SERVICES

How to Master
the Art of Selling
FINANCIAL SERVICES

by Tom Hopkins

Made for Success
PUBLISHING

Made For Success Publishing
P.O. Box 1775 Issaquah, WA 98027
www.MadeForSuccessPublishing.com

Distributed by Made For Success Publishing

Your Compliance Department's instructions regarding sales practices for representing products to clients and potential clients takes precedence over the content in this book. Before implementing the phraseology used in this book it is important that the reader consult with the Compliance Department of his or her organization to assure that the phraseology meets with the organization's guidelines.

Library of Congress Cataloging-in-Publication data

Hopkins, Tom
How to Master the Art of Selling Financial Services
p. cm.

ISBN: 978-1-61339-803-6
LCCN: 2015906046
   1. Business & Economics / Sales & Selling / General
   2. Business & Economics / Finance / General
   3. Business & Economics / Training

Printed in the United States of America

For further information contact Made for Success Publishing, +1 425 526 6480 or email at Service@madeforsuccess.net

About the Author

Tom Hopkins is recognized throughout the world as America's #1 sales trainer. He has taught, motivated and inspired millions of individuals directly through his public seminars and as a consultant to some of the most prominent companies and organizations in the world. These include many of the top firms in the financial services industry. His books, CDs and DVDs have sold in the millions and Tom Hopkins International, Inc. is one of the leading sales training organizations in the world. His books include How to Master the Art of Selling (Grand Central Publishing), having sold over 1.4 million copies, Selling For Dummies, Sales Closing for Dummies, Sales Prospecting for Dummies (Wiley), Sell It Today, Sell It Now with Pat Lieby (Tom Hopkins International) and The Certifiable Salesperson with Laura Laaman (Wiley).

Hopkins' real-world training in sales began in the challenging arena of real estate when he was just 19 years old. During his first six months he earned only $42 a month. After realizing that selling was a learned skill, he invested his last $150 of savings in a selling skills seminar that saved his career.

After becoming a dedicated student of the profession of selling and applying what he learned, he sold more than $1 million worth of $25,000 homes. During that phase of his career, he closed 1,553 property transactions—365 of them in a single year! Many of the sales records he set then still stand today. By the age of 27 he was a self-made millionaire.

His success brought with it challenges. He had a huge fear of public speaking yet was asked to speak when receiving his many awards. Not knowing what else to say, he spoke about how he made the sales that earned him those awards. Rather than sitting idly listening to his speech, audience members began taking notes! Seeing the light of understanding on the faces of those in attendance was the spark that lit the way to his true path in life—teaching.

In addition to conducting more than 60 seminars per year, Hopkins is a pioneer, innovator and leader in the production of top-quality audio and video training programs, powerful presentations that are continually being updated to provide the most relevant information and techniques for the current economy as well as for a variety of industries and selling situations.

He is a long-standing member of the National Speakers Association. And, he is one of its few members to be honored with its Council of Peers Award for Excellence.

Hopkins' extensive real-world business experience, keen insights into the art of selling, down-to-earth approach, understanding of financial services consumers, and sense of humor make him uniquely qualified to teach you **How To Master the Art of Selling™ FINANCIAL SERVICES.**

Acknowledgements

No one can teach who has not learned. First and foremost, I'd like to thank the professional financial advisors who have come into my life to assist me on a personal level. From them, I've learned volumes and benefited tremendously.

Second, thanks go to the hundreds of thousands of students of my training who work diligently in the financial services industry—a very necessary and growing field.

Third, much appreciation goes to the many companies in the financial services arena who have hired me to assist their consultants, representatives and associates with their selling skills.

And last, but certainly not least, thanks go to my team at Tom Hopkins International for their diligence in keeping our training top of the line.

Other Titles by Tom Hopkins

How to Master the Art of Selling

The Official Guide to Success

Low Profile Selling

Mastering the Art of Listing and Selling Real Estate

Selling for Dummies

Sales Prospecting for Dummies

Sales Closing for Dummies

Sell It Today, Sell It Now—The Art of the One-Call Close
(with Pat Leiby)

The Certifiable Salesperson
(with Laura Laaman)

Table of Contents

Introduction

It was my very good fortune that my first exposure to the financial services industry was a positive one. Don Zeledon was an insurance agent who contacted me when I was in my early twenties. Being young, I thought I didn't need insurance. Don was patient and listened to all of my excuses, diversions and stalls. Then, he educated me with examples of unfortunate situations in which other young families like mine had found themselves. He appealed to my intellect, but especially to my emotions and my sense of duty in caring for my family. He persuaded me that having a life insurance policy was less painful than what could happen to my family if I didn't have one.

As my real estate sales career took off, so did my need for the services of financial industry professionals who could help me protect the investment properties I owned, advise me on putting my increased earnings to good use, help me avoid financial pitfalls and so on. Again, I was truly blessed by the professionals who came into my life, educated me and helped me make wise decisions. So, I applaud you for choosing to serve the needs of others as a financial services professional.

Let me tell you a little bit more about my history so you'll understand what this book offers you. I once did physically demanding labor lugging steel around construction sites. Seeking something better, I discovered the exciting and liberating the world of selling. Selling is by far more mentally demanding than many other careers, but with greater potential for satisfaction and reward.

The key word is *potential*. There are no guarantees. You're only as secure as your last sales call and your own ability to educate people.

I had no guarantee when I entered the field of residential real estate sales that I would succeed, but I knew it would afford me a better opportunity to generate a good income for my family than construction. What I didn't understand was that even though I wasn't afraid to meet and talk with people that skill alone wasn't enough.

After a pretty awful first six months in the business, it finally dawned on me that I should start asking questions of the other agents who were doing well. What were they doing that I wasn't doing? I quickly learned that succeeding in sales requires a very specific set of skills. But I also discovered that they were skills that could be learned. That's when I became a voracious student of the nuances of selling. I made the subject of selling my passionate hobby.

By investing in self-development and in proven-effective sales training, I entered a phase of my life where much of what had previously been turning into muck and mud, started turning into silver and gold. By working hard to professionally serve the needs of as many clients as possible, I achieved levels of success beyond my wildest dreams.

As I travel around the world today conducting sales training seminars, one of the most frequently asked questions is how I achieved such a high level of success in my real estate career. For example, my last year in real estate, before becoming a sales trainer, I set a record of having 365 closed transactions in a single year. That feat was possible because of the excellent team of professionals who helped me—one in the title insurance field, another in the financial arena, and the third in escrow services. My clients and I relied on these folks to see that all the details regarding their dreams of home ownership were handled properly. Seeing the joy and peace of mind these people experienced because of our combined services was truly a highlight of my life.

Then, I hit my next roadblock. As good as my skills had become when working with clients one-on-one, I had a gargantuan fear of public speaking. As much as I loved winning awards for my sales volume, I hated being asked to give speeches when the awards were presented.

Fortunately, I had a mentor who was the best sales trainer around. I had attended so many sales seminars with J. Douglas Edwards, always sitting in the front row, trying to write down the words as he spoke them, that he and I struck up a great friendship that lasted the rest of his life.

When I told Doug I had turned down a request to give a speech about how I achieved success he said, *"Tom, you must do what you fear most if you want to overcome the fear."* I took those words to heart and went from being a student of selling to becoming a student of public speaking. With determination and hours of practice, drill and rehearsal, the fear was overcome and a desire to help others master selling skills was born.

It's my goal now to show you how to experience the incredible satisfaction of helping others through your financial services career. I want you to see the light of understanding dawn on the faces of your clients when they realize the value of the service you provide. Then, you will earn the income level of a champion financial services professional and all the benefits it will bring to you and your loved ones.

If you got into this field because of the income potential, you're smart. It's there, but the highest incomes will only be earned by those who exceed their clients' expectations when it comes to providing service. You see, the word *service* comes before the word *success* in every aspect of life...even in the dictionary!

Mastering the art of selling involves mastering the craft of providing your clients the education, products, services, and personal contact before, during and after the sale that they want, need and, more important, deserve. That's how you succeed. That's how you'll not only survive and grow in this business, but will thrive, prosper, and achieve greatness through it. And like a good ride on a first-rate roller coaster, you'll enjoy it.

Believe me. I've ridden that roller coaster and hung on through major ups and downs that negatively impacted my selling career, others that pounded our sales training business, and still others that affected the global economy. The solid selling skills covered in this book are the foundation of my success and they can be yours as well.

My company and I have been teaching proven-effective selling practices to professionals in the financial services industry since the release of my first book, *How to Master the Art of Selling*, in 1980. We've had the privilege of helping to make a difference in the future of the world as families and individuals enjoy the peace of mind that comes from knowing they've made wise choices to protect their families, build wealth and plan for long-term retirement.

You may be wondering if the content of this book talks about your specific products. I know the industry is broad and includes every-thing from basic life insurance to intricate retirement and estate planning strategies. But, regardless of the product there is one common denominator—people. Yes, you sell financial products, but to whom? People. You are first and foremost in the people business. The skills for working effectively in the people business are covered here in detail and in a way that lets you start putting those skills to work immediately. Get your product knowledge from your company. Get your *"selling products to people"* skills here.

This book was written to customize the most requested topics from our general sales training to the financial services industry. I encourage you to make it a working tool, one that you continually refer to for information, guidance, help and inspiration.

- Fold the page edges so you can easily find important passages.

- Use a highlighter or underline material that strikes a chord within you.

- Take notes in the margins, or use flags and Sticky Notes.

- Read it, re-read it several times and really use *How to Master the Art of Selling Financial Services* to build, enhance and sustain your career in this exciting field.

Take what you learn here to achieve the goals that are most dear to your heart by providing superior service to your clients through professional selling.

_____

"The empires of the future are the empires of the mind."
- Winston Churchill

CHAPTER 1

Mentally Preparing for Sales Success

Congratulations! You have chosen a career in one of the best fields of all times. I mean that. Money really does make the world go around. Those who are wisest with their money have opportunities to enjoy more of what our world offers, including more fun, more security, and more wonderful opportunities. And you have chosen to become well-educated on financial products to earn a very nice income for yourself while serving the needs of others. By picking up this book, you have come to the right place to begin. I've always been known as a foundational teacher so we're starting at the ground floor.

Speaking of ground floors, we'll use a building analogy throughout this book. None of today's great architects would begin a structure without a complete set of blueprints. Follow their example. Do not attempt to build your business without developing your own personal set of plans to arrive at the final completed structure of your dreams.

Take Advantage of the Advantages

Before we get into creating your career blueprint, let's consider some of the greatest advantages of this exciting, challenging and most rewarding field. Why is this industry the best place for you?

Advantage #1 – Nearly everyone is a potential client.

Unless you plan to specialize, such as working only with the affluent who have $10 million or more in net worth or some other niche, your pool of potential clients expands to nearly every adult on the planet. Think about it. Who doesn't need knowledge and sound advice on keeping and growing their money? It doesn't matter if their discretionary funds are only $50 or as much as $50,000 a month, everyone has a need for what you offer. Millions of people are seeking to earn, save, invest, and increase their fortunes. They need life insurance, debt consolidation services, long term care, annuities, 401K plans, full blown investment programs and other financial services. Most will have a continuing need for those services and so will their families as the children grow and are told, *"Just call Bob/Sally. He/She has taken good care of us for a long time. You'll do well with them, too."* Your legacy will grow with continual referrals from satisfied clients.

Advantage #2 – You, and only you, determine your income level. You get to choose how hard you work, how long you work and how many clients you want to work with. You also choose how well you'll develop your skills.

Some of the best advice I ever got about selling as a career is this: *Selling is the highest paid hard work and the lowest paid easy work there is.* That's it in a nutshell. If you're willing to work hard, the reward is huge. My job in this book is to help you learn how to increase your income and your sense of accomplishment by working smarter as well.

Sure, you can double your income by working twice the hours and with twice as many clients. The real fun begins when you develop your skills to a point where you're working half the time and still making the same income. Or, if you choose, you're working the same amount of time for double the income! No one limits your income potential in this field but you.

NOTE: It doesn't matter how well or not-so-well you've done so far in your financial services career. You are to be commended for investing in your financial future by owning this book, by investing your time to read it, and by applying its tactics and strategies to create a better life by better serving your clients. You are already demonstrating your desire to go beyond average to achieve "champion" status.

Advantage #3 – You'll experience real joy and satisfaction in helping others throughout your career. Who doesn't want that as a reward for their daily toil? If you're in this business for the right reasons—to serve the needs of others—it'll warm your heart every day that you help a family or an individual take one more step toward doing the right thing with their money because you educate them. You help them make wise decisions to protect their families and their assets, to start investing for growth and planning for the future. You're making a powerful, positive difference in people's lives. What a bonus!

I'm constantly amazed at the shockingly high percentage of our population that hasn't the foggiest idea of capital, how it works, and how it can be used to better one's life. This is where you come in. You are an integral component of our free enterprise system. Your knowledge, wisdom and experience with financial matters puts you in a position to help fuel the dreams and ambitions of individuals, families, companies and organizations—it's how you make things happen.

Advantage #4 – You are in charge of your time. Of course, most financial planners work specific hours but you have the freedom to choose those hours and the flexibility to include important non-work activities in your schedule. There are few things worse than achieving business or financial success while losing touch with the loved ones who make the rewards worthwhile.

Most folks in the financial services industry are entrepreneurs, or independent contractors who work on their own, but not alone. They align themselves with large companies or groups whose products they offer. Those companies have your back. They provide education, service and support for what you do, but they don't dictate your hours. You inhabit the very best of both worlds.

Advantage #5 – You can live and work practically anywhere on the planet. It's wise to build your business and your reputation in the community in which you live. However, if you choose to specialize in another market, or even another part of the country, once the accounts are established, much of your continuing service can be done via phone, email, and online.

Advantage #6 – Providing financial services is mentally stimulating. It's important to remember that the industry is large and diverse. With so many choices to explore, you are bound to find aspects of the industry that are a good match for your skills and interests. Rather than being a Jack or Jill of all financial trades, you may decide to specialize in working with particular lines of products. And, with the needs of your clients and industry offerings constantly changing, you'll find yourself enjoying learning about new products that may be beneficial to your existing clients or help you earn the business of new ones.

In some ways, your job is to gather just the right materials and equipment (products and services) to build the dreams of your clients. You are a financial structural engineer!

Advantage #7 – There's long term potential. The need for financial services professionals is huge. It's on the Bureau of Labor Statistics list of "in-demand" occupations. In fact, the Bureau of Labor Statistics estimates for the ten year period from 2006 to 2016, 2.2

million positions will be necessary in financial services. See...what you do is necessary for the long haul. If you're willing to do your part, you can build a lifetime career in this field. A large number of industries are dwindling, downsizing or dying every year, but financial services is not one that's even on the edge of extinction.

If you'll look up other statistics, you'll likely find that average financial services counselors and representatives earn good incomes. That's wonderful news but my goal in this book is to show you how to rise above average—how to earn whatever income you set your mind to.

I don't know of anyone who has ever taken my training with the goal to become average. There was a time when mediocrity was acceptable. It was the standard—the norm. Achievers were seen as being pushy and aggressive. Or, worse. Many were considered oddballs. Not so today. Go-getters are admired and their progress watched. Clients want to work with someone who's on the cutting edge of the industry. They want to be the first to know about new products that might benefit them and they'll go out of their way to work with an advisor who has his or her fingers on the pulse of the financial world.

Improve Upon the Law of Averages

Even if you were born into an average family in which no one ever earned more than an average level of income, or if they never stepped out into the entrepreneurial world that doesn't mean you can't. You just have to choose to leave those old thought patterns behind and adopt new, more progressive, more rewarding ones. We've seen this in the movies where the average Joe or Joanne aspires to greatness beyond working in the mines, the mills, the manufacturing plants or whatever. They succeed because of their hard work and determination. They rise above the expectations others have for them by thinking differently, then acting upon those thoughts. You see thoughts really do become things.

I once heard the late great Earl Nightingale say, *"You are and will become that which you think about most of the time."* Acting upon that single sentence, changing what I thought of myself, has made all the difference in my life. I was able to rise above the old me—little Tommy Hopkins who was not good in school, who was afraid to stand up and speak in front of the class, and was picked on for his small stature—to achieving a life I had previously thought an impossible dream.

I hope you have people in your life who are supportive of your career choice, but if you don't, know that it's possible to have whatever you want in life anyway. You just have to choose your own way. Then, act upon that choice. Mr. Nightingale was absolutely right. Action always follows thought. Think right. Act right and you'll get the right results—every time.

Find new friends and associates who will support your dream of success as a financial planner, counselor or representative. That doesn't mean ditch your old friends, though you may end up spending less time with them. It just means to stop allowing their choices and their expectations of you to limit what you do for yourself.

How do you do that?

Well, you can start with something as simple as affirmations. An affirmation is a positive declaration about something. It's a statement of belief.

Here are some examples:

"I'm happy. I love my life. I'm always discovering fascinating new things to do."

"I know that I have a wonderful future."

"I work smart and deserve all the success I want."

This process involves the use of self-talk. It's the conversation you have with yourself. It's always going on in your head whether you consciously realize it or not. These thoughts represent your core beliefs and they're what made you what you are today. If you want to be someone different tomorrow, you need to start actively, consciously, talking differently to yourself. I know this sounds overly simple but it really is that easy. The hard part is that you have to decide what messages you want to give yourself and you must review them consistently until you catch yourself having those positive conversations in your head.

The more specific you are the better. Invest 15 minutes envisioning your perfect life and writing out its description in positive statements. The key is to make certain as you read each statement that it provides you with a clear picture of that life.

Our minds think in pictures, not words. For example, if someone says the word "car" to you, you may picture a Ford while the person standing next to you "sees" a Lexus in his or her mind's eye. So, the more descriptive your words are the better your picture will be. And, the better, the clearer, and the more real your picture, the better your real life becomes.

The key to your success with affirmations is belief. You must believe in the power of affirmative statements for that power to enter your life. If you lack belief, say them anyway—regularly and sincerely. In a surprisingly short amount of time the proven positive results of your efforts will make a believer out of you.

Here are some sample affirmations you may want to use as they relate to your career:

"It's amazing how easily I meet new people who need my services."

"I'm terrific at remembering names. I remember a new person's name right away."

"I'm always excited to learn about the newest products I can offer my clients."

"I keep in touch with my clients on a regular basis so they know I am here to serve."

Keeping Up Appearances

Now that we've addressed what's going on inside you, let's take a moment to consider the exterior. I won't dwell or ramble on here, but I feel the need to address the issue of your personal appearance as it relates to your image as a financial services advisor people will want to do business with.

Do yourself a favor. Get dressed as if you're meeting a typical client and step in front of a full-length mirror. Look at yourself from head to toe. Adjust your posture if you feel the need to do so. Smile. Then, ask yourself this question: *"Would I entrust something as important as my family's financial future to the advice of this person?"*

If you feel even the slightest sense of doubt creep into your mind, make a phone call immediately to a hair stylist, someone to give you a manicure, or someone to provide advice on a professional wardrobe. Shine your shoes. If you're a man, learn how to iron your shirts so they look crisp. Learn how to tie a better knot in your tie. If you're a woman, consider visiting the experts at the make- up counter in your local department store. You have to look as sharp as you are mentally.

You and I know that it's your knowledge people really want, but if you don't look like you have taken your own advice and appear financially successful, why would they? Appearances do count when working with the public.

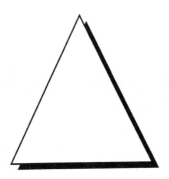

The Groundwork

Okay, let's get back to our blueprints. Before a structure can be built, the ground must be measured, tested for density, and in some cases worked over a bit to be level. The groundwork in selling includes a basic understanding of what I call the selling triangle. The triangle is not unlike a pyramid—one of the most sound structures man has ever created. Talk about standing the test of time! I'll speak about all three sides shortly, but let's begin with the beginning, the base.

Attitude, Enthusiasm and Goals

The foundation of your business includes your attitude, enthusiasm and goals. You see, you can have all the product knowledge in the world and excellent people skills, but if your attitude is sour and you're not enthusiastic about what you're doing, you might as well not bother getting out of bed in the morning. Your lack of enthusiasm will show. Worse, it's contagious. If you're not upbeat and excited about what you do for people, they won't be either. If you don't engage their emotions, they won't do business with you.

As a comparison, think of a doctor with a poor bedside manner. He may be very knowledgeable and skilled, but if he doesn't excel at making his patients feel they've made a good decision by seeing him, they're not likely to return. They'll find someone who makes them feel good about feeling good.

Your positive attitude is what you feel within and your enthusiastic manner is what people see on the outside. They should come not only from your belief in the service you provide but from the goals you have set and are working to achieve.

Let's say you have a goal to do what every red-blooded American family wants to do—go to Disneyland. You've done the research and know how much you need to earn and save to achieve the goal by a pre-determined date in time. Your family is excited. You're excited. You want to be the hero and achieve the goal. You know that providing excellent service to a certain number of clients will do the trick. Are you excited to get up and get to work every day? You bet you are! Are your spouse and kids excited for you? Are they telling you how great you are to be helping other people so they can benefit, too? Yes and yes.

That's your foundation: Attitude, Enthusiasm and Goals.

Evaluate each of those areas right now. How do you feel about what you do? How is that feeling showing up in your outer world? If you're not satisfied that they're as good and as strong as they could be, perhaps you need to set better, loftier goals.

The goals you set must be better than your best, but believable. Otherwise you won't stretch and grow. You won't be motivated to achieve them. Let's take a moment to review the basic laws that apply to goals:

1. <u>Your goals must be believable.</u> If you don't really believe you can achieve it, you won't. End of story.

2. <u>Your goals must be clearly defined.</u> If you set a physical fitness goal regarding weight loss, you wouldn't write, *"I'm going to lose weight."* Why? Because nobody wants to "lose." They want to gain and in this case you want to gain a healthier body. So you'd write, *"I'm going to achieve my ideal weight of 175 pounds by November 6th, 2009."* It's clear. It's specific and it has a deadline. Great goal!

3. <u>Your goals must be ardently desired.</u> You simply won't work for something that "would be nice to have or do." Your goals must be ardently desired. I love that phrase because you nearly have to grit your teeth to say it. It just doesn't sound right if you say it without emotion. You must be passionate about your goals.

4. <u>Your goals must be vividly imagined.</u> This goes back to our discussion of what you see in your mind's eye. Can you envision yourself at 175 pounds in the summer? What are you wearing? How do you feel at that weight? Get as vivid a picture as you can. See it. Smell it. Feel it. Taste it.

5. <u>Your goals must be in writing.</u> This seems to be the most daunting task for people. Too many feel that if they put a goal in writing and don't achieve it, they will have written proof of their failure. If that's your thinking, stop it right now. The value of putting your goals in writing is so you can read them over and over again to keep them fresh in your mind on days when everything you touch turns to something other than gold. Your written goals are your motivators to keep moving forward. And it's okay if you change your mind or alter your goals as you journey toward them. They're not stamped in concrete after all. But do put them in writing. It's an important step toward making them real.

That takes care of the foundation of our selling skills triangle. Now, let's take a look at the sides.

Product Knowledge

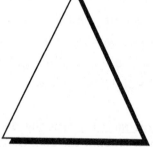

On the left side, we have product knowledge. As I already mentioned, this is something you get from the company or group you're associated with. Since you're now treating your business like a hobby work is now fun. One of your goals must be to study all of the product information you can get your hands on. After all, it will do you no good to stutter and stammer your way through information on something you want your clients to own.

"Oh, yeah, Mrs. Johnson, we have this new product that's exactly what you need. Let me find the brochure on it. It's, uh, oh, I don't remember exactly how they describe it, but it sounded like it would take care of your concerns about..."

If you don't know it, don't try to sell it! You won't come across with confidence and they won't have confidence in either you or the product even if it is great for them. You must be seen as a truly knowledgeable and competent professional within minutes of meeting any new prospective client. The potential client must believe you not only can *"talk the talk,"* but that you can *"walk the walk."* This requires study, rehearsal and may even involve conversations with others who are marketing the same product to get a better feel for the type of client it will help the most.

Financial products are changing all the time to meet changing consumer needs. Government regulation of the industry requires you to stay on top of what you can and cannot do or say within this realm. If you don't keep up and follow the ever-changing rules, you may find yourself out of touch, out of the office because you're in court, or worse, out of business.

To stay on top of the knowledge game, attend as many educational sessions as you can reasonably fit into your calendar. Join an industry trade association and read the newsletters and other information they publish. It's their job to provide the latest information. It's yours to read, understand and internalize it.

Now, let's move on to the right side of our formidable structure and what the rest of this book is all about—your people skills.

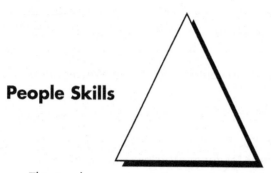

People Skills

This is where you put your great attitude, your enthusiasm for your products and your product knowledge to use in achieving your goals. As a general overview, people skills involve: finding ideal potential clients for your products; how you meet them; strategies to qualify them about their needs; skills to educate them; methods to address their concerns; a course of action to get their business; and, to earn the right to ask for referrals.

You may already be strong in some of these areas. Most people who get involved in a career in financial services enjoy meeting new people and getting to know them. They may also be good at explaining new ideas and concepts to others. Those skills are essential to giving effective presentations. The goal of the following pages is to help you understand that there is a step-by-step process to effective selling and to teach you where your existing skills fit in. For those areas in which you may not be as skilled, we'll cover very specific, how-to strategies for taking those steps in the most productive manner.

Before we begin with our selling steps, let me give you one bit of advice. If you truly want to improve where you are right now, it will take some dedicated effort on your part. You will need to commit to read this entire book not once, but several times. In fact, most of our students have found it most beneficial to read our books a minimum of six times to gain solid retention of the training. Don't panic! I'm not telling you to read it six times through over and over, though that's not a bad idea.

Rather than overwhelm you with directions of how to proceed, make a commitment to live by the following twelve words that have made all the difference in my career and the careers of millions of my students.

I must do the most productive thing possible
at every given moment.

That's it. Simple, isn't it? In fact, you could probably memorize that sentence right now if you just repeat it to yourself six times. That little sentence is something I have lived by for many years. I've encouraged others, like you, to do the same and it's amazing what happens. If you ever find yourself stuck on a plateau in your career, stop doing whatever it is you're doing. Take a moment to consider if what you're doing is the most productive thing possible. If it's not, make a new plan and move on with energy, enthusiasm and confidence.

It's probably not productive to work on analysis of your client's financial information during times when you could or should be talking with clients directly. Plan your time to do those things when it's most productive.

Many people have a fear of planning their time. They think if they plan it all out and something changes the schedule their world will come crashing down. It doesn't if you plan correctly. Plan for client time, analysis time, study time, time to reflect on what you're doing right, time to consider where and how to improve, time to rest, time to take care of your personal needs, and quality time to invest with your loved ones. (Please note, your loved ones shouldn't be last on your list of how to be productive with your time. If you do put them last, you may find yourself financially successful but with no one there to share the rewards.)

Those twelve words above can be the most profound source of direction for you in wise time management. Obviously, since you're still reading, you must consider this time most productively used for learning new ideas for selling more effectively. Let's get on with it!

"Service to a just cause rewards the worker with more real happiness and satisfaction than any other venture of life."
~ Carrie Chapman Catt

Chapter 2

Prospecting-Finding the People to Sell

Prospecting is the art of finding the right client for your products and services. It's a two-step process:

- Finding the people to sell.

- Selling the people you find.

Here, There and Everywhere

If you want to find potential clients, just follow the lead provided by a song from The Beatles, *"Here, There and Everywhere."* That's precisely where they are. That fact presents more of a challenge than an opportunity if you're cold calling. Of course, in selling financial services, looking here, there and everywhere will have you bouncing left and right, up and down, and back and forth like the metal ball in a pinball machine. Warm prospecting is a wiser course when marketing investments, insurance, financial plans, peace of mind, and the joy of anticipating favorable returns.

Friends and Family. Start by contacting your friends and family. These folks know, like and trust you. If they don't, you might consider a line of work where you can survive as a loner. Hopefully, they'll be excited that someone in the family is picking up some expertise they don't have themselves, but can benefit from. They should want to pick your brain and use your services.

As a bonus, they will have their own network of friends, acquaintances and co-workers. Some will surely be in need of your financial skills and the products and services you offer, if not now probably in the future.

Here's an example of how warm prospecting can work.

You have friends who are in all sorts of professions, but do you consider them sources of business leads? I'll bet it never crossed your mind. In fact few people who market a product or service realize the wealth of warm prospecting opportunities they already have or encounter on a regular basis.

Extend your prospecting antennae. Everyone you know knows other people—lots of them. Never again leave a meeting, whether you're giving or receiving service, without considering who this person might know that needs your services.

Acquaintances. Speak to those who are just *acquaintances*, as well. You cross paths with a lot of people every day. Some will need your product and some will know of others who can benefit from your service. I bet you haven't a clue as to how many people you meet (or could potentially meet) every day. Mentally walk back through today or yesterday and trace your footsteps. Did you stop at the coffee shop? Did you drop off a prescription for a refill? Did you eat lunch somewhere besides your home or your desk? Did you pick up your kids at soccer practice? Or, drop them off? How about on the way home from work? Did you run an errand? Could you have?

Every one of those situations brings you into close encounters with other people traveling in similar paths. Stop running on auto- pilot, reach out and meet them.

Prepare a 30-second "commercial" about you, your product and your service ready so you can use it at a moment's notice when you make a new acquaintance. And then be sure to use it.

> *"Hi, I'm Hank Martin. I help people achieve their share of the American Dream by providing professional analysis of investment opportunities so you can be certain your money is doing exactly what you want and need it to do for you. I guess you could say I show families and individuals ways to save and make money, thus, eliminating debt and building toward financial independence."*

Suppliers. Other businesses offer great opportunities for prospecting. Work hard to impress every business you hire or purchase from. Word of mouth is one of the most powerful forms of advertising. When respected business people recommend you, other people listen.

Itch Cycle. Take advantage of what I call the itch cycle. Every product or service has a limited lifetime. Bonds mature. Term insurance comes to an end. A five-year financial plan doesn't automatically roll over into year six. Contact clients before the product "winds down" so you can be there to pick up the business when they need to renew. Or, guide them to another product that's right for the next phase of their lives.

For example, if you notice that the bond market is easing into a decline, it's a good idea to contact the individuals and families you know who have purchased bonds to discuss the possibility of investing in the rising value found in the stock market or vice versa. Not only will you be improving your own business, you'll be providing genuine service to people in real need.

"Mike and Martha, that investment plan we drew up for you last year met your needs at that time. With how quickly things change in our lives, we recommend an annual review to assure that your strategy is on target to meet your continuing needs.

Also, many new products are released each year to help investors like you improve their planning. I have a few suggestions to make concerning your particular situation. Why don't I pop by for a visit to discuss some of the great opportunities that just might fit your needs today especially well?"

Stay on top of things within your industry. It's an unalterable law of nature that things change. When you see changes in the economy, in financial services or housing regulations, in the local business environment, in lending laws, in trends in the financial services industry or in anything affecting you and your clients, act on that knowledge. Make contact to see if there are any ways you can be of service regarding the coming change. You'll not only be providing service, you'll also be cementing your image as a pro-active (with the emphasis on the prefix "pro") expert in the field.

<u>Orphaned Clients.</u> See if any clients have fallen between the cracks. If you work for, manage or own an organization of any real size you will develop a substantial list of clients. As people come and go in your organization, it's likely that some of those clients will be dropped or forgotten. These people, who are familiar with and who should be happy with your product and service, should be excellent potential clients for additional products and services. Check with your employers, your co-workers and company records to see if you can begin working these hidden gold mines.

The Media. Study the media. Regardless of your market (local, regional, statewide or national) there are newspapers, radio and television programs, magazines, newsletters, web pages and other media providing information that can propel your new business efforts to ever greater heights

News reporting, by definition, focuses on the negative. As they often say, *"We don't report on planes that land safely."* That's a good and legitimate point, but the news can have a serious negative impact on the way people think. They can become convinced that all the news is bad and that now just isn't the time to invest in financial services. Of course, negative thinking leads directly to negative results. They could easily find themselves in need of the very services or products they were too afraid to purchase.

Address those fears carefully and with thought, but head on. No matter how bad the news may be, there is always some good news somewhere that can be used to provide balance. Also, negative news could itself be used as a reason to get involved. After all, if the economy is shaky, what better time to look for wise financial counsel?

Read, watch or listen to the news to discover the "movers and shakers" in your industry and community. Notice who is being promoted or who or what company is moving into town. Make an effort to add them to your list of contacts. This isn't as challenging as many folks think. Most people are surprisingly accessible. Pick up the phone and make the call. Introduce yourself. Set up informal or even formal meetings to get to know them one-on-one. Offer your services. And if someone is new to the community, offer yourself as a reference guide to that community. The important thing is to commit to meeting new people—all the time. Learn their needs, and put yourself in a position of showing how your product or service perfectly meets those needs.

Suppliers. Your suppliers can provide more than supplies. They are likely to live in the area and know a lot of people. They are aware of information you probably will never acquire. For example, he or she might have heard that Mr. Monroe down at Acme Deluxe Manufacturing has just gotten a promotion and a substantial bonus.

He and Mrs. Monroe might just be in the market for a solid investment in which to put that new money to work.

The Three-Foot Rule. Consider anyone who comes within three feet of you as a potential client or referral base. I'm serious. It's part of the here, there and everywhere philosophy. If appropriate, strike up a friendly conversation and within it roll out your 30-second commercial. You'll be surprised at how many people need or know someone in need of your services.

The Internet. Reach clients by reaching out through the Internet. You can quickly and easily acquire an amazing volume of information on virtually any subject by logging online and tapping a few key words into your computer. You can thoroughly research entire industries, specific companies and organizations, and even individual officers of a corporation all from the comfort of your office.

Reach out through the Internet by creating your own web page so prospective clients can quickly and easily research and contact you. When you set up your web page be sure to reference it every- where you can— on your business card, letterhead, advertising, signage, public relations efforts and so on. Make it easy for people to find you.

Signs. One of the best places to advertise to a captive audience, and I really mean captive, is on your automobile. Think about it. When you're stuck in freeway or highway traffic what do you have to look at except other cars? Well, the people in those cars you're looking at just happen to be looking back. Why not give them a little reading material to break up the monotony? Those metallic advertising signs that slap against your car door are economical and easy to acquire.

I've found sources for all types of products and services while sitting in my car. Imagine if someone needing your product or service looks out his or her window to see your name, your company name, address, e-mail address, and phone number and the fact that you just happen to have the solution to the financial question they were just pondering. That little sign stuck to the side of your vehicle could easily be the cause of a new client becoming "stuck on you."

<u>Emerging technology.</u> Some years ago companies prospected by mailing printed brochures. New and affordable technology arrived and many of those companies began sending out "brochures" on video tape. Then CD and DVD "brochures" became the rage. The Internet has revolutionized the way many companies and individuals conduct business. Many are prospecting through web pages and e-mail campaigns. These are all valuable and proven tools for prospecting. Use them when appropriate for your marketing needs. And realize that some other new technology is currently in development. When it arrives, use it if it's right for you.

Create a Network

A network is a group of individuals who help each other achieve their individual goals. I help you get where you want to go in business and you in turn help me get where I want to go. That help can come (and probably will come) in many forms.

For example, you may be new to setting up your own business and need the advice of a professional lawyer, accountant, real estate broker or any number of suppliers. One or more people in your network can probably make a few solid recommendations. You don't have to reciprocate in kind either. Later on that person may require help writing a speech for his or her business-contact group. If that's one of your areas of expertise, jump in and offer to help draft the speech. The point is to help each other in whatever area each person needs that help as long as you both know why you're doing it.

It's important to think of your network not so much as a mutual aid society, but more as a group of on-going relationships. It's not a matter of "I owe her because she helped me." It's "how can I help you...what do you need...what can I do for you." As with anything else, the more you put into the effort the more you will get out of it.

If you don't have a network, create one. It's fun and you get to meet a lot of great people in the process. And don't limit yourself by in-the-box thinking. Just because financial services is a white collar industry, don't think you can't have blue-collar members in your network. The mechanic at the automobile dealership, your mail carrier and people in any number of occupations you can name can all help and be helped by your network.

Once you're in a network remember success depends on mutual cooperation and support. It's a two-way street in which you give as good as you get. Share the wealth of information, leads and contacts and you will reap the wealth of information, leads and contacts. Here's a sample scenario between you and Joe, the service technician who maintains your copier.

Joe: "Okay, Mrs. Henning. I've given your copier the full once-over, changed the toner and tightened a bolt here and there. It's good for another hundred thousand copies."

You: "Thanks, Joe."

Joe: "I appreciate your business. How are you doing?"

You: "Fine, just fine. But I'm always on the lookout for new clients to serve."

Joe: "That reminds me. We just got some good news. My sister and her husband are having another baby. I know they'll be needing more life insurance and I'll bet they haven't even thought about a college fund yet. I know they'd be interested in talking to you."

You: "Would you mind giving me their full names and phone number?"

Joe: "Sure thing and give me one of your cards to pass along to them. I'll be seeing them later this week."

There's one last area that applies not only to "all of the above" topics, but really to all topics, your entire career. It's the matter of trust. People will not do business with people they do not trust. Yes, people get snookered all the time, but how much repeat business does the dishonest person get? How many referrals does he or she earn? And consider the effect of word-of-mouth on that person's future transactions, business and livelihood. People talk and word always gets around. When you cheat someone, the biggest victim is yourself. Build trust and you will build business.

You can't earn trust by being ethical during church or at the synagogue and then breaking the rules at work. Hypocrites do not do well in this business—not for long. Earning trust is more than a process—it's a lifestyle.

In my book *Sales Prospecting for Dummies®* I devised an "Ethics 101" test. I'd like you to apply that test whenever you face something that might challenge your trustworthiness. I promise, it will help keep you on the right path.

- Would I want someone to do this to me?

- What would I do if someone did this to me?

- Can anyone get hurt if I do this? Who and to what degree?

- Can I look Mom and Dad/the preacher/my mentor/ my kids in the eyes when describing this action?

- Would I be proud to see this on tonight's news program?

When so challenged, think about it, even for a few seconds. Think like a champion and you'll know what and what not to do.

Target Your Target Market

Often the here, there and everywhere potential clients create a serious and daunting challenge. Narrowing your focus so you can concentrate on a specific, well-defined target market is one way to make sure you're seeking only the best and most potentially rewarding "turf." Here's a simple process to do just that. It works equally well for individuals and organizations.

Begin by listing your top 25 to 30 clients. Look for commonalities among them such as age, income level, education, financial needs, probable needs in the future, ethnicity, hobbies and interests, and so on. Once you've completed the exercise, see how well they match up to your own profile. Note any common patterns.

Analyze each client. Write down the size of their investment funds, financial service needs, insurance needs, outstanding loans and financial commitments, property ownership, how they came to use your service, who referred them, if they have provided you with referrals, and so on. Again, note any common patterns.

Next, list your top 25 sources of referrals. Analyze them also. Make note of any common patterns between yourself and your sources. Be careful not to get so deep into this analysis that it takes you all day. You should be able to see the pattern emerge with a quick review.

The patterns that emerge should provide the necessary information for you to narrow the focus of your prospecting. You may discover a valuable niche market that you can readily serve. For example, although you may be concentrating your efforts on approaching one area of business, you may discover a profitable niche in another, such as serving small suburban businesses with net incomes of under $1 million, young families with the breadwinner just moving into middle management and a higher salary and benefits package, or individuals who focus on asset protection rather than building wealth. The needs are limitless. Use your imagination. Where are the people you can best serve?

Again, opportunity is always here, there and everywhere if you are willing to put in the effort to find and profit from it. I highly recommend that you conduct this exercise soon. You'll quickly discover whether or not your marketing efforts are on target.

Find the people. Provide the service. And you will be astonished at the rewards that will enrich every phase of your life.

"We must not sit down and wait for miracles. UP and be going! "
~ John Eliot

Chapter 3

Sales Readiness

Once you start implementing your prospecting efforts, you need to check your level of readiness for actually meeting with someone. To win in sales, you develop a game plan, you practice, hone your skills, apply knowledge, psyche yourself up to deliver your presentation with enthusiasm, and prepare to give each potential client contact the proverbial 110 percent of effort.

You will be preparing yourself to perform all of the people skills we covered in the first chapter, but there are some other skills that are important, too.

Memory. Names, places, dates, facts and figures are important. So are the attitudes and beliefs of our potential clients, their interests, likes and dislikes, wants, needs, goals, hobbies, the names of their kids and grandkids and so on. The better your "memory bank," the better your own bank account will be.

Of course, no one can remember everything, but everyone can improve his or her memory. Read books on the subject. Buy or rent CDs and DVDs. Train yourself daily by making a game of memorization. Make an effort to remember as much as you can about the events that occur in your everyday life. The payoff will astound you.

Remembering names is especially important in selling situations. Two ways to help remember someone's name are (1) repeat the name at least four times during your first encounter and (2) associate that name with something so you can "jumpstart" your memory quickly the next time you meet.

"Glad to meet you, Mr. Planner. My name is Victoria Bell."

"I'm glad to meet you, too, Miss Bell.
(Thinking Liberty Bell...Liberty Bell...Liberty Bell).

There's no need to go into the "why" of this technique. Just know that it works, so use it and you'll never be embarrassed by forgetting a name again.

A Second Language. In the Western world, more than in most other countries, we are nations of immigrants and sons and daughters of immigrants. You'll find pockets of people from foreign cultures in various neighborhoods especially throughout the United States and Canada. Diversity is one of the factors that makes our two countries so rich in culture.

Learning the second or third language predominant in your market will help you understand and better serve the financial needs of those potential clients. And when word gets out among their language peers that you are fluent and truly understand them, your referral base will grow exponentially.

It's not a bad idea to consider taking classes or tutoring in the culture and language from someone who lives in one of those areas. That type of education will provide a down-to-earth feel for it rather than classes offered through a college or municipal program though they are not bad choices either.

Communication. How you say something can be as important as what you say. The manner in which you use the gift of your voice will often determine the success or failure of your efforts to serve your clients. It's something people always notice on their initial contact with you.

Some people speak informally while others will be so formal as to be stiff. Some speak quickly and in short bursts while others may actually drone on using long sentences and exaggerated mannerisms. Learn to match your vocal inflection to theirs. It is imperative that you do this as quickly as possible so they will feel at ease with you as they come to like you and trust you.

Voice is particularly important when on the phone where you don't have the option of backing up your statements with body language and facial expressions. People have a natural ability to hear what you're really saying regardless of your words. If your voice lacks excitement, your potential client will believe you lack conviction. If you're distracted by your computer screen or paperwork on your desk while speaking with a client, they'll sense it on the other end. They'll know they're not receiving your full attention. This type of treatment will cause them to lose faith or worse, lose trust in your ability to make their needs and their business a priority. Potential clients who feel that way often seek out other, more professional financial services providers. Don't risk it! Record a few phone calls, with permission, and study how well you use your voice on the phone. You'll hear how you can improve how you sell over the phone.

You can also match "vocal" inflection in written documents. Pay attention to any letters, memos or e-mails you receive from potential clients and adopt a similar style in your replies. Most importantly, always assume what you put in your letters or email messages might be forwarded on to someone else. For that reason I strongly recommend that you err on the side of formality.

Yes, you can SHOUT, *get noticed*, **create attention** or ***CREATE A LOT OF ATTENTION*** in the printed word. You aren't a hypocrite when you adopt someone else's style of speech or writing. It's just a means for better and more efficient communication. And please don't "cuss" by writing $#&&!!!@ to emphasize a point. Cursing, in whatever form, is inappropriate. Champions don't work that way.

Here's a good tip when establishing a relationship with a new prospective client. Ask, *"How do you prefer that I stay in touch with you?"* It's a simple and easy step that few in the industry ever bother to take. Some people prefer person-to-person contact. Others prefer phone calls, e-mail or faxes or some combination of methods. Ask the question and respond from then on appropriately. This simple act of courtesy will put you head and shoulders above the rest.

Public Speaking. Addressing groups such as business clubs, civic organizations, your child's class or scout troop accomplishes three key objectives.

> *One, public speaking increases public awareness, not only for your business but it increase your name recognition.*

> *Two, increased awareness of you increases your business volume.*

> *Three, public speaking builds confidence. The more intimidated you are by public speaking the more you need to seek out and take advantage of speaking opportunities. I know this can be a daunting task but remember, I did it. I really do understand.*

Yet I can tell you once the fear is conquered the benefit from the confidence you gain is immeasurable!

If you have mastered some or all of the skills we've covered here, congratulations. Now, work on improving them. If you haven't mastered them, pick one and work on it until you do. And then pick another and another and another until you are confident with all four.

Fear Producing Words

The vocabulary we use tells others a lot about us. Few people are likely to give conscious attention to analysis of our individual words, but their subconscious will. Every word really does create a picture in the mind's eye. Those pictures generate emotions. Unfortunately, much of the typical jargon most people in sales use generates the negative emotion of fear. Words can be some of the greatest fear-inducing factors blocking any salesperson's hopes of gaining new clients.

Over the years I've developed a set of "Fear Producing Words" and a list of "Replacement Words" that temper the fears created by the other words. Let's cover the really scary fear producers and the replacement words and phrases we've tested over the years. They really do make a difference. You'll see. I'll explain them here but give you a "cheat sheet list" to assist with your memorization of them later in the chapter.

<u>Sell or sold.</u> No one wants to feel that he or she is being sold something. That implies manipulation. Never say, *"I've sold six of these policies already this week!"* That may be great for you, but doesn't make the clients you're speaking with feel special. Everyone thinks they are different. Their situation is unique. They have certain expectations about their involvement with a financial professional. You must meet those expectations. You are here with these people to serve

their needs. To assist them. To help them acquire or get them involved in a program that is ideal for their particular set of circumstance. So, your replacement words for *"sell"* or *"sold"* are *"help them acquire"* or *"get them involved."*

> *"John, Mary, once you get involved with this program specifically designed to meet your needs, you'll find yourself experiencing more peace of mind than you have now about your financial future."*

A third option might be to help them *"get started"* since your first sale should be a product or service that initiates a long term relationship. People prefer to be involved in their acquisitions, especially one as emotionally important as investing their money. Your goal is to have them feel they're partners in the process—not just recipients.

<u>Contract.</u> Contract is one of those words that sets the red flags flying. It sounds so permanent, confining and legal. The replacement words of *"paperwork,"* *"agreement,"* or *"form"* convey the same meaning without causing alarm.

> *"Kathy and Bill, you don't mind if I draft up your feelings on the paperwork as we talk, do you?"*

<u>Cost or price</u>. The words *"cost"* or *"price"* create a mental image of outgo rather than income. Certainly everyone understands that purchases require money. However, the softer terms of *"amount"* or *"total amount"* have been proven less fearful. People work hard for their money and it is understandable that they're loath to let it go. The term "amount" is lighter and softer, but gets the same meaning across.

> *"I think you'll agree, Harry, that the amount we're looking at is within your budget."*

Down payment. Again, the frightening words convey not only the down payment, but year after year of additional payments. The replacement words of *"initial amount"* focus attention on a single amount to get started with the long-term benefits they want to own.

> *"To get started with the optimal scenario for your particular situation, Barb, only requires an initial amount of $200."*

Monthly payment. Again, breaking the total amount, which may seem overwhelming, down into manageable *"monthly amounts"* puts the purchase in a more realistic and acceptable light.

> *"Connie, Dave, to gain the peace of mind having the right amount of life insurance protection your monthly amount is just $150."*

Buy. This is another term that creates an image of money leaving bank accounts, wallets, purses. Replace it with *"own."* People want to own the benefits of future financial protection for loved ones. They just don't want to "buy" life insurance or annuities.

> *"You're going to be excited after you own your annuity, knowing you'll have consistent amounts of money available to you when you retire."*

Deal. A deal can be good or bad. We're all looking for them. Yet a truly "good deal" is seldom found. Effective financial direction, when followed, provides excellent *"opportunities"* and should be considered wise *"transactions."*

> *"Paul, you will be so happy you took advantage of this excellent opportunity to make a difference in the lives of your children as they start thinking about college."*

Objection. Objections are a way of stopping forward motion. When a potential client objects, it's like they're putting the brakes on. If you're sensitive to the impact of words you may feel an actual physical movement as if you were riding in a car that stopped abruptly. Seasoned professionals know that objections are little more than a tap of the brake to consider a change in direction. Start referring to objections as *"concerns"* or *"areas of concern."* They are much friendlier terms. A concern is something that should be addressed—a continuation of the conversation.

> *"I can appreciate that concern, Michael. Would you mind elaborating on it?"*

Problem. There are no problems, only challenges that can be addressed and overcome. Even if you say something like, "Our goal is to overcome any problems you might be having," you're pointing out something negative in a negative manner. Instead, refer to problems as *"challenges."* A challenge is something people get excited about, attack proactively, feel they have the possibility of overcoming.

> *"Our goal is to eliminate any challenges that are currently keeping you from achieving the financial peace that you desire."*

Pitch. Pitch has really become a negative term, one implying shady or shifty salespeople selling inferior products. Justified or not, that's how people think. Use *"presentation"* to soften the image.

> *"Carolyn, Dan, I'm confident at the end of my presentation you'll be excited about what our company can do for families like yours."*

Commission. Eventually, you will encounter someone who will understand just enough about the business to know you're earning money from their decision. Even though they want the benefit of your advice and service, it may bother them enough to bring it up. They may come right out and ask you how much commission you make on their business. Rather than let this fluster you, address your remuneration as a "fee for service."

> *"Fortunately, the companies I work with build a fee for service into every transaction and you can rest assured that the service you will receive will far outweigh any fee. That's what you really want, isn't it, Gary?"*

Do you see how nicely that covers the situation and turns things back around to the quality of service your client wants? It's all in the words.

Sign. Parents the world over have told their children, *"Never sign anything."* We all have that ingrained in our brains. Smart financial planners never use that word. Replace it with these: *"approve," "okay," "endorse,"* or *"authorize."* These terms have the same meaning, but don't raise the same fears.

> *"With your approval right here, Craig, we'll get you started on your own personal road to financial recovery."*

Appointment. Appointment carries with it the connotation of commitment, which can turn off many potential clients. Use *"visit"* or *"pop by and visit."* A *"visit"* is so much warmer and less intimidating.

> *"Mrs. Garrett, I was hoping to just pop by and visit with you regarding something new our company is providing folks like you and Mr. Garrett."*

<u>Cheaper.</u> Cheap these days implies shoddy products. When making a financial commitment, the last thing anyone wants is cheapness. They do want the most economical situation possible. Use the words *"economical"* or *"more economical."*

> *"Frank, I'm recommending the most economical solution possible just to get you started on a sound financial program."*

<u>Customer or Client.</u> Those two words are most often used in retail situations. Financial services should be envisioned as a higher solution. Replace those words with these phrases: *"the people we serve"* or *"the families we serve."* We want to establish long-term relationships with these people and these terms better express that feeling.

> *"We have been fortunate to serve hundreds of families here in the local area. We're proud to know our services are making a difference in their lives."*

<u>Referral.</u> Referrals are a key to your on-going success, but to make sure that success is on-going use the term *"quality introduction."* Names and addresses are fine, but you'll experience considerably greater success when your client personally introduces you to a new potential client.

Fear Producers	Replacements
Sell or Sold	Get them involved
	Help them acquire
	Get them started
Contract	Agreement, Paperwork, Form
Cost or Price	Amount, Total amount

Down payment	Initial amount
Monthly payment	Monthly amount
Buy	Own
Deal	Opportunity, Transaction
Objection	Concern, Areas of concern
Pitch	Presentation
Commission	Fee for service
Sign	OK, Approve, Authorize, Endorse
Appointment	Pop by and visit
Cheaper	More economical
Customer or Client	People we serve
Referral	Quality introduction

Words are essential tools of the trade. Never underestimate their power to close sales or to lose them. Choose your words carefully.

Step Right Up to Selling, Serving and Succeeding

You are always selling—yourself, your company, your reputation, an opportunity to meet with someone face to face, an opportunity to present the value of your offering, your financial products, your professional service and so on. The first step toward closing the sale and establishing a long-term mutually beneficial relationship with any client is to get the opportunity to walk through their door or to get them to come through yours. Opening those doors requires preparation for and the completion of several steps. In all, there are seven:

- Greeting

- Introduction

- Gratitude

- Purpose

- Appointment

- Telephone thank you

- Letter or e-mail thank you

Before getting into more detail on those seven steps, I want to pass along three tips for insuring a successful call.

First, at all times be courteous. At this stage you do not know your potential client well enough to tell a joke, discuss politics, talk about religion, or call him or her by a first name. You may never reach a point with some clients where it will be wise to talk about religion or politics. Leave those topics up to your clients to bring up. However, beware of why they begin those conversations. Be prepared with a polite, neutral answer that won't offend should they try to evangelize you with regard to either subject. You must be on your absolute best behavior to even have a chance at achieving the best outcome.

Second, be willing to do whatever is necessary to get that all-important face-to-face meeting. That's where you'll do most of your actual selling. Unless your potential clients are piloting the Space Shuttle, physically ill or otherwise involved in something that makes meeting impossible, you must use your skills to get an in-person meeting so you can in turn use your selling skills to serve their needs.

It's important that you develop a thick skin for this step in the selling process. Initial rejection isn't personal (unless it's from mom and dad), so don't take it that way. Be persistent and keep on performing like the champion you are.

Lastly, when you get agreement on the meeting, reconfirm the details. Send a brief letter, send an e-mail confirmation, or make a pre-meeting phone call, but make sure your prospective client remembers the time and place of your visit.

In the pre-meeting call, you want to try to eliminate any opportunity for them to re-schedule or cancel. You do this by telling them how excited you are about the strategy you've come up with to meet their needs and how much work you put into preparing for the meeting. Once they realize the obligation you've made to meeting their needs, they'll be more likely to follow through with the visit.

Now let's see how we can climb those seven steps to serving your client successfully.

Step #1. Greeting. Your greeting sets the tone for the entire conversation and possibly for the face-to-face meeting as well. Again, be on your best behavior. Say "good morning" (afternoon or evening). State the name of the person you want to speak with using his or her full name. Do not use the person's first name unless you are already on a first name basis. Also, never, never, never try to sell your product or service during the greeting. Save the selling for the visit, which is the real goal of your call.

Step #2. <u>Introduction.</u> Be brief. Be positive. Be confident. State concisely the nature of your business. Suppose Mr. Patterson has just lost a bundle on a bad investment. He's scared, embarrassed, in shock, at the end of his rope, and probably hasn't a clue as to his options.

Right away state the nature of your business, hint that you might be able to provide some relief or at least options for any lack of financial peace of mind, and put him at ease because you're not calling to "sell" anything.

Step #3. <u>Gratitude.</u> I've often noted that two of the most powerful and least used phrases are "please" and "thank you." Always show gratitude to the other person for taking your call. Keep your tone conversational and don't rush.

Step #4. <u>Purpose.</u> State the purpose of your call. *"If I could show you a way out of your current situation that would not only provide you with peace of mind, but actually get you started on the road to building real wealth, would you be interested?"* Of course he would, he's hanging by an emotional (and possibly a financial) thread at the end of that rope. More people than you can imagine are in the same or similar situation. Again, keep your tone conversational. You're not some slick huckster swooping in to take advantage of his misfortune. You're a hero coming in to save the day and show him how not to repeat his past bad experience.

Remember, that your call is actually a fishing expedition. You're not selling anything; you're trying to gain information that will help you sell during a face-to-face meeting.

Step #5. <u>The Visit.</u> This is the heart and soul of your entire call. You want to set a definite time and place for a meeting. Generally, you're better off asking for a short period of time. Twenty minutes is the most frequently requested time period. (You'd be astonished at how much real selling you can do in that amount of time when you're well prepared.) Twenty minutes doesn't sound like much of a commitment to the potential client. And, once you're together and the presentation is moving along professionally chances are he or she will be so intrigued and impressed that you'll easily be able to extend the meeting as long as necessary.

Don't expect the other person to offer a date and time to meet with you. Offer a choice of times. *"Would 9:10 tomorrow or 2:40 Thursday be best for you?"* Note the off-hour times. I recommend them because they're easier for the potential client to remember than on-hour time frames and they show that you are very time conscious. If neither of those times is acceptable, continue offering choices until an appropriate one is found.

Step #6. <u>Telephone Thank You.</u> This is where you offer another thank you and reconfirm the time, place and date for the meeting. Get accurate directions to wherever you'll meet. Confirm those directions later yourself by checking a city map, using an online service such as Google Maps®, or even by driving to the location a day or so before the meeting.

If the meeting will be at your office, provide very clear directions, including cross streets and which corner your building is on. Even give the color of the building if it stands out and you're in a collection of professional offices. Do this in a friendly, conversational manner, as if you were telling a friend where to meet you for lunch. Remember, people who agree to meet with you could be under a lot of stress about their situation or at least nervous about the financial commitment they could be facing. They could be easily confused in such a state of mind. Make it easy to be found.

Step #7. <u>Letter or Email Thank You.</u> If the meeting is more than two days away immediately write a thank you letter that reconfirms the time, date and place of the meeting. Keep it brief, polite and professional. Use your business letterhead and include one of your business cards. Also consider including a map or driving directions from the potential client's starting point if the meeting is at your office. This follow up letter has a psychological benefit in that it makes the upcoming face-to-face meeting "real" in the mind of the other person. It confirms a commitment they've made and should honor.

Another good idea when working with potential new clients is to call them the morning of the day of the agreed upon visit with a quick reminder. Even if you get their voice mail, that's okay. Your goal is to demonstrate professionalism. Express your excitement for the time you'll share and promise to be on time.

It's a Question of Questions

If you don't ask the right questions in the right manner your potential client won't answer with the information you need to properly serve his or her specific needs. It's your responsibility to gather all the information on what they already have in place that relates to the client making a decision to go ahead with your recommendations.

Prior to your potential client's arrival, perhaps in your phone conversation or in the thank you/confirmation letter, list the information or documents he or she needs to bring to the meeting. This information might include:

- A recent statement from their current investment provider

- A list of all current investments

- Copies of his/her last two paychecks

- Information on any other sources of income

- Bank statements

- Information on debts

- Any written financial plan or goals

- Projected windfalls (an inheritance, for example)

- Current insurance policies

- Known future expense estimates (college, for example)

- Any other specific information relative to your products and services

Don't expect people to have any of this information readily at hand. Say that you understand that it may take a bit of searching to pull it all together. *"It's quite normal not to have that sort of information right at your fingertips."* The last thing you want to do with a potential new client is to make someone feel uncomfortable, disorganized, or worst of all, stupid. One of your first and most important tasks during an initial meeting is to put them at ease so they can quickly see your professional qualifications and start liking and trusting you.

Master Selling by Mastering Service

I want to close out this chapter with a few tips for providing genuine service. That commodity is so rare these days that those who practice it are quickly recognized as outstanding professionals in their fields. Trust me. Word gets out. Over time people start avoiding the scam artists, the mediocre performers, and the also- rans. They gravitate toward the champions who achieve incredible heights by putting their clients first. Here's my six-point plan for taking care of business the champion way.

1. Get "in" with the "in" crowd and the "in" crowd is made up of the real achievers in your community. Join that group so that you'll be supported and you will support the best of the best in your business community.

2. Dance with the one who brought you. That's an old country saying full of wisdom. Remember the people who have helped you up the ladder of success once you achieve that success. Find ways to return the favor by helping them achieve their goals. Look for opportunities to promote your associates, clients and your friends in business.

3. Always have and show empathy toward both potential and satisfied clients. You must really care about these people and their challenges. Empathy is something you can't fake. People will see right through fake sincerity, mark you as a phony, and seek service from a more genuine and client-focused professional. Be real. Be honest. Care.

4. Don't think of your competition as the enemy. Some of my best business leads come from competitors who are unable to serve the needs of a specific client. Because we maintain good relations and friendly competition, they never hesitate to recommend me for business they can't serve. I make it a policy to return the favor. Knocking the competition is guaranteed to mark you as an amateur. When people are considering new financial services providers, they want to work

with the best professionals in the area. Sure, a champion beats the competition hands down in most cases, but he or she is never shy about offering a hand to a friendly competitor.

5. Never become complacent. Always be on the lookout for new potential clients wherever you are and whenever you can. Nearly every face you see in a crowded shopping mall has or will have a need for some type of financial service, probably several types over time. When you begin looking at every person you see as a potential client, it changes your perspective on your business. It will show in your outward appearance and actions and will attract new business your way.

6. Look for ways to improve your product so you can improve your service. Pay attention to the challenges you find most common among your clients. If quite a few are expressing the same concerns, pass that information upward in your company. There may be a specific product available that your firm doesn't currently handle, but could if they only knew the need was there.

Okay, we've just committed our first potential client to meeting with us. What's the next move? Well, let's turn to the next chapter and see how we create a successful first meeting.

"With self-confidence fulfilled, you'll find that folk have confidence in you."
~ Goethe

Chapter 4

Original Contact—Introducing Yourself to Your Next Sale

Original contact, step two on the people skills side of *"How to Master the Art of Selling FINANCIAL SERVICES,"* is a key element in our foundation of great selling. This is the stage where you meet a potential client face-to-face and make such a positive impression that things start happening in your favor. Original contact is the point at which you send out such positive "vibes," that you radiate such confidence, and you are so obviously intent on solving the challenges facing these folks, that they begin to like and trust you. I can't say this enough. Remember, people will not willingly do business with someone they do not like and trust.

You'll earn that trust by demonstrating in word, body language, attitude and deed that you really do care about helping them achieve what they want. You'll prove that you are fully capable of handling that task. You'll build rapport and begin a long-term mutually beneficial relationship.

Again, do not try to sell your product or service at this point. To do so is to act prematurely and you'll possibly frighten people away or at least put them on edge. The first 90 seconds of this meeting are crucial. That's when the potential client will size you up and make a hard-to-change decision about you, your character and your reliability. Look the part of the successful provider of financial advice and services you are. This is where their foundation of trust is laid.

You Fear Less or They Fear More

A lot of salespeople have an unnatural fear of meeting new people. For some reason it scares the heck out of them. But do you realize that potential clients arrive at the meeting with you bringing their own set of fears? No matter how much your mental knees are shaking, chances are their fear is so great as to make yours seem minuscule. Think about it. Of the two of you, they're the one making the greater financial and emotional commitment. You're concerned about gaining their trust (and their business), but they're facing a long-term and perhaps a lifetime commitment with their money. No wonder they're scared. Understanding their concerns will help you calm your prospective new clients and counter their fears so these folks can clearly see the wisdom of doing business with you. As a provider of financial services, the greatest enemy you'll ever face is fear – yours and theirs. In a way you have a common bond, albeit a "shaky" one.

Even when you're past the prospecting point with your clients, you will still have to face Mr. Fear every time their situation changes and you have to present new financial concepts to them. Always assume that Mr. Fear walks in the door when meeting with potential new clients. He also arrives with current clients who are coming in for a program overview or to learn about a new product or concept.

You'll overcome those fears by proving that you are professional, knowledgeable, concerned and sincere about serving their needs. Arriving at this state will take a different amount of time for different people. Every person, couple, and family is unique, as is every selling situation. Some will be reassured after your smile and friendly handshake. Others will take a lot more convincing that they should go with your recommendation for their financial needs. Here's a list of common fears you'll have to address.

1. <u>Your potential client is at first afraid of you and what you might do.</u> I know that's irrational because you are a champion and you're there because you sincerely want to help them arrive at a sound decision that is to their benefit. However, your prospective client doesn't know that until you prove it. The fact that you're a salesperson is enough to send shivers down the spines of a lot of good people. Again, of the two of you, they're the one making the largest commitment. Respect that. They've likely heard second- or third-hand horror stories all their lives about friends and relatives of "someone" who has been taken advantage of by slick, self-serving unprofessional people in this industry. Add to that all the negative imagery they've been hit with for generations in books, magazines, movies and television, no wonder they're skittish.

You'll be surprised to find this same fear in friends and relatives who sit down at the table with you. Suddenly it's not Tom, the nice boy down the street, helping Bob and Betty Carter. It's us vs. him. That's totally wrong, but that's the situation we must face. My thinking is that we're hit with this attitude 99 times out of a hundred.

How do we overcome it? First, get over your surprise and accept it. Next develop your people skills so you can quickly and straightforwardly put your prospects at ease. When they're relaxed and comfortable, they're in a better position to listen to you, see the sincerity in your every word and deed, and come to like and trust you. Build rapport. Ask questions and show that you're interested in what they are saying. Don't tell them you're trustworthy; show them through your words, vocal inflection and body language.

2. <u>Your potential client is afraid of making a mistake.</u> You know how foolish you felt when showing off your new suit (stereo, car, fishing rod, fancy dress) only to be met with polite snickers or in some cases friendly ridicule from your friends. Imagine that fear magnified by the thought of committing large sums of money for your products and advice over time, perhaps decades of time. You can donate the shoes, the stereo or the fishing rod to a worthy cause, but you can't box up an insurance policy, an early penalty for withdrawal investment, or a long-term investment program and leave it at the Goodwill donation center.

The key to overcoming this fear is education. The more you show your potential clients the wisdom of their decision and the more they come to understand, the less fear you will have to overcome.

3. <u>Your potential client is afraid you'll lie.</u> You know you're not a liar. The people who have done business with you know you're not a liar. People in your network know you're not a liar. Your potential clients look at you as a total stranger. It's like the old Western movies, in their minds a stranger in town bodes ill. The way to address this fear is to get past being that stranger. Use your product literature, positive coverage in the news media, testimonial letters and referrals. It's that old "outside expert" way of thinking. If someone else says you're okay, then you must be okay. That's the value of testimonials – and of earning those testimonials.

4. <u>Your potential client is afraid of making money commitments.</u> We've been brought up in the United States with an overwhelming fear of debt—of having piles of bills each month or having our money spent before we've earned it. Remember that debt is a relative term. It means one thing to a mega corporation investing pension funds in the stock market, but it means something else entirely to a young family

buying its first life insurance policy or trusting a share of their small savings account to a financial advisor.

Reinforce the wisdom of their decision to get involved with a financial strategy. Explain the benefits of your product and the value of the service you and your organization will provide.

5. <u>Your potential client is afraid of losing face.</u> This fear is closely aligned with the fear of making a mistake because when you make a mistake, your friends and relatives are likely to hear about it sooner or later. Here's an important point to consider. If the clients lose face it's your fault. At least in their mind it's your fault. It's much easier to blame you than it is to admit to fouling up. Handle this by continually reinforcing the fact that you and your clients are working together to achieve their goals. You are providing a valuable, much needed and much wanted service.

6. <u>Your potential client is afraid of the unknown.</u> This is another area where education is the key to success. The professional manner in which you make your presentation about the benefits of your product will help them face their fears and see that those fears are totally unjustified. When the unknown becomes known, fear disappears.

7. <u>Your potential client fears repeating a bad past experience.</u> There's an adage that applies here. *"Fool me once, shame on you. Fool me twice, shame on me."* If someone has been involved with an unprofessional salesperson in the past, you may pay the price in the p resent. Again, educating your client on your product, your company, the proven value of the service you offer is essential. Provide information. Offer proof. Ask questions to find areas of legitimate concern that must be addressed and address them. You must serve your potential client even before he or she becomes your client!

8. <u>Your potential client is afraid because he or she has heard negative comments about you, your company and/or your product.</u> This negative third party information may be due to a misunderstanding, a questionable competitor, or for some other incorrect, irrational or misunderstood statement. It doesn't matter what it is. If your potential client believes something negative about you or your company, it's fact until you prove otherwise. This is another area in which your product literature, favorable news coverage, and testimonials play a key role. You may even want to directly involve satisfied clients to help make your point.

The bottom line – just as you face fears in making or not making the sale, your potential clients have fears about entering and concluding the sale. As a champion salesperson, it is your duty to overcome the fears on both sides.

You can do it. Fear less. Be fearless.

How to Begin an Original Contact in Five Easy Steps

We have five senses: sight, smell, touch, hearing and taste. These senses are tools that help us become winners in our own eyes, in the eyes of our company, and in the eyes of our clients. Each sense is individual, but they all work together to give us a better, more accurate picture of the world we live in. In much the same way we, as professionals selling financial services, have the use of five techniques that allow a potential client to acquire a better, more accurate picture of their world with us in it. These techniques are:

1. Smile and mean it.

2. Make eye contact.

3. Offer a greeting.

4. Shake hands.

5. Provide your name and get your potential client's name.

Your potential client starts sizing you up the first second he or she sets eyes on you. If you're in a large lobby and the walk across it takes some time, the potential client may have formed a firm impression before you even get to say "hello" or offer a handshake. If you're dressed inappropriately, are unkempt, shuffle or shamble across the room, have poor posture, appear intimidated or over- confident, and so on, your opportunity to win the day may be over before it even begins.

You have about ten seconds to make a good first impression.

If you're a bit nervous at first meetings, don't be alarmed. It's natural to feel a few "butterflies" in your stomach. Even the top performers get that sometimes. I don't mind a small onset of "nerves." It's nature's way of keeping us on our toes. If you ever lose that slight uneasiness you're probably getting complacent and that means you're about to make a lot of mistakes and will probably lose a lot of sales. If you're nervous before an original contact, relax. That's S.O.P. (Standard Operating Procedure).

I still get butterflies before going on stage and I've presented nearly 5,000 seminars in my training career. The butterflies are there because I truly care to give the best performance I can with each and every audience.

If you stop having butterflies, take note of your attitude. Has it changed? If you get to where you don't truly and sincerely care for the people you serve, you will have lost your edge in this business and it will show. There's another side to the butterflies as well. If you continually get so knotted up that you feel as though you'll throw up on your potential client's expensive carpet, perhaps it's time to rethink whether or not you're in the right business. You may need to sit down with your manager, partner, or suppliers and go over your product knowledge and/or review the selling skills training you've had thus far before meeting with many more clients.

Selling financial services isn't for everyone. If you determine that this most wonderful of careers just isn't what you're cut out to do, that's okay. You're better off getting out of the profession and moving on to something more productive and personally rewarding rather than making yourself ill by trying to force something that just isn't right for you. However, if you can get those butterflies flying in formation, you'll do just fine.

Don't just hear. Listen with all the attention you can muster. Hear the words being spoken, but also note the equally valuable messages being sent through body language, vocal inflections and even pauses in sentences. Be sure to let your potential client know you're listening through the use of proper verbal and body language responses. "I see," "I understand," and "Yes" are each extremely effective when uttered at the proper time

Nod in agreement when appropriate. Lean forward. Make eye contact. Listen with all your senses carefully attuned to your potential client.

Translate what is being said. Sometimes the other person's words and his or her real meaning are at cross purposes. That's one of the reasons why reading body language is so important. You have to learn to "read between the lines" during a conversation. Don't hesitate to clear your thinking by asking appropriate questions. *"If I'm hearing you correctly, you're saying that at present you have absolutely no written, long-term financial plan. Is that right?"*

It's important that you and your clients stay on the same page and ultimately that's your responsibility. Also note that you always need to speak in language people understand. If your client doesn't nod and respond quickly to a question, think about whether or not you're using industry jargon. Rephrase your question in layman's terms. Never assume that because someone has a college degree, is a professional in some field, or is obviously a very intelligent person, that he or she comprehends the language of your industry. You can't stay on the same page if your prospective client is constantly trying to refer to a mental thesaurus.

Evaluate what you are translating as you translate it. Continue asking questions if necessary, but make sure you understand everything said, verbally and physically. Don't hesitate to take notes during a presentation. Taking notes shows that you are really listening, that you pay attention to details, and that you're thorough — all excellent qualities for someone selling financial services.

Respond to what the other parties are saying. At this point you should be in a position to determine whether or not you have a legitimate potential client. Phrase everything you say so that it emphasizes the benefits of your services. Even if the other person turns out not to be a good client candidate, you can still ask for a quality introduction. Good service generates the opportunity for more good service – even when you don't close the sale.

An essential step in any client contact is to also get referrals to other potential clients. I'll defer discussing that at the moment, because the topic is covered in Chapter Eight, *"Getting Referrals."* For now, just note that you should always ask for referrals when talking with potential clients whether the potential client is qualified or not. Remember, a champion does not actually use the word *"referral,"* preferring the much friendlier and more powerful *"quality introduction."*

Smile and the World Smiles With You

You can tell a lot about a person's character by the way he or she smiles. Is it a sincere smile? Or fake? People do not like or trust phonies and they certainly don't want to do business with them.

Use your entire face when you smile and make sure it's genuine. It invites the potential client into the process, puts him or her at ease and gets your original contact off to a good start. A great smile can quickly and easily break any pent up tension in the room. As we mentioned, chances are your potential client is as nervous as you are, probably more so. Making the process easy on him or her makes the process easy on you. And that's the beginning of a win/win outcome.

You might be surprised to learn that smiles do not come easily to some salespeople. I've known delightful outgoing people with a great sense of humor who have lousy smiles. Some folks have it naturally and some just don't. If you're in the latter category, practice half an hour a day before a mirror. Work on smiling and on smiling quickly and naturally. You'll feel awkward at first and if anyone in the house happens to walk by they'll probably think you've finally taken a long walk down the short pier of sanity. Believe me, though, it's worth the effort.

A great smile is an invaluable asset and one of your most powerful sales tools. Forget the old advice to grin and bear it. A champion grins and enjoys it.

An Eye for an Eye

"The eyes are the window of the soul." That's absolutely true. Making eye contact with your prospective client is one of the most effective ways to begin the process of building rapport and trust. Eye contact is an essential element of positive body language. The eyes are perhaps the hardest element for a liar to disguise because our eyes and how we use them "speak" a universal language. Think back throughout your life to the times people have lied to you. Didn't they look down or look away while stating their lies? Of course, except for highly trained con artists, and some teenagers, most people can't look someone in the eye and tell a lie.

Even if you're the most honest person in the world, if you can't look a potential client in the eye he or she will think, even if it's subconsciously, that something is wrong, that you're not telling the truth or that you're holding back some of the truth. You must develop the ability to make comfortable and confident eye contact if you want to succeed in selling financial services. If you have been somewhat shy up to this point in your life, start out by looking at the lower edge of the other person's forehead or at the bridge of the nose. At least you'll be looking in the right direction. Making eye contact will become easier the more you work at it.

Don't let making eye contact turn into a visual contest to see who'll blink first. Your potential client could become uncomfortable and refuse to purchase your offering. Never lock on to someone's eyes for an extended period of time. Some people interpret that as a threatening act. Smile, make eye contact for a few seconds and then glance away at your notes, his or her paperwork or something else that's relevant. If you don't, you might win a staring contest, but you'll probably lose an opportunity to close a sale.

Great Greetings Lead to Great Results

The simple act of saying "hello" may seem basic and an obvious way to start a conversation. Still, I have seen salespeople so anxious about giving their presentations that they sail right into it without so much as a "how-do-you-do." A proper greeting is not only common courtesy, it's a sound and professional business practice.

Which form of greeting you choose and the vocal inflection you use to state it depends upon a number of factors. Obviously, you won't use the same greeting to a new potential client as you would with an existing and long-term client, a relative or the friend you spent that lost weekend in Mexico with.

For example, you'll want to use a more formal approach with anyone you meet for the first time. *"Gladdaseeya"* isn't part of a great greeting. As the relationship matures you'll most likely move on to more informal greetings – but only if your potential client is comfortable with informality. As mentioned before, stick with Mr./Mrs./Ms. until you get permission to use their first names.

Shake Hands and Come Out Selling

A handshake is usually an important element of a greeting. Most people expect it and would be offended if you didn't. Some people are just shy and do not enjoy shaking hands. Others like and want to shake hands. Some actually fear or find the process unpleasant. And some want to shake hands, but can't for some extenuating circumstance.

How can you figure out which is which?

Well, there's a simple technique I've found that's quite effective. Keep your right arm by your side and slightly bent. This signals the other person that you are ready to shake. If he or she reaches out, complete the action and shake hands. If the other person doesn't reach out, you're not in the awkward position of reaching out too eagerly and you can simply drop your arm or use it to direct the other person to wherever you'll be seated for the visit.

Don't be offended if someone doesn't shake hands. People have all sorts of reasons for avoiding the gesture. Some folks are just shy and find touching other people awkward or even unpleasant. Every once in a while you'll run into someone with arthritis or a broken or bruised hand. He or she could find shaking hands a physically painful experience.

When a handshake is appropriate, here's how you do it right. Reach out and grasp the other person's entire hand and shake with a firm grip. Don't try to impress the other person with your strength by crushing his or her hand. Don't go to the other extreme and offer a weak grip either. Be like Goldilocks and find a grip that's "just right." Keep the shake brief and make eye contact while doing it.

If meeting with a married couple, it's important that you shake hands with both parties. If they have a child with them, shake his or her little hand, too. It will make the kid happy and you'll impress the parents. Never tussle a kid's hair or tweak his or her cheek. They hate that. Didn't you when you were a kid?

Play the Name Game

You must get two specific names right in the first moment of a prospecting call: yours and theirs. They must know your name right away and they must remember it. *"Hello, I'm Tom Hopkins. I'm so glad to meet you today."* Make sure they hear it and get it right. There are few things more awkward than correcting a potential client who has gotten your name wrong. *"That's interesting, Mr. Hoskins. Tell me more about your company."* Suddenly you're no longer presenting, you're correcting. The "spell" (and perhaps the sell) has been broken and you may have to make extreme efforts to get your presentation back on track.

Obviously, you'll want to get the name of your potential client correct. If it's an unusual name, it's perfectly okay to ask for the proper spelling and to write it down in your notes. *"Pratt, that's with two 't's, right?"* They'll appreciate your attention to detail and your desire to get things right—sought after traits in someone providing financial services.

Becoming friendly with your prospective clients is necessary, but be wary of becoming overly friendly too early. If Mr. Pratt's first name is Charles, do not make the mistake of saying, *"Glad to meet you, Charlie."* Don't automatically call John by the familiar Jack, Theodore by Teddy, or Elizabeth by Liz. It's impolite and it marks you as being unprofessional.

Follow the lead of your potential client. Wait for her to say, *"Call me Liz."* Follow this guideline throughout the getting to know you stage of selling. Things, and your clients, should warm up by the time you get to the qualification or presentation stage. If they're still not allowing the use of shortened or nick names, it's perfectly acceptable to ask. *"Mr. Pratt, as we move forward, I want you to be as comfortable with me as possible. Please call me Tom, and may I have your permission to call you Charles?"*

If you've heard a spouse or friend call him *"Charlie,"* you should ask permission to use that form of his name. Far more often than not, he'll agree. Or, he might say, *"Chuck is fine."* If not, again, follow the potential client's lead. Use the form of their names they prefer. Always, show respect and courtesy. People notice, appreciate and respond to it. Most people expect it and they're right to do so.

By following these simple steps you can assure yourself of a successful beginning of the original contact stage, the next step in our selling skills foundation.

Taking It Easy Makes It Easy

I've seen some salespeople in financial services so intent on controlling the sales process that they act like demanding choreographers training young dancers for a Broadway show. "Five-Six- Seven-Eight! Dance-Dance-Dance!!!" Dancers, military recruits, and members of the high school marching band may respond to that kind of direction. Prospective clients will respond by finding another sales- person. Yes, the salesperson has to control the process, but you don't and can't do that by being pushy or demeaning. You do just the opposite and put your prospects at ease and doing everything you can to make the process an efficient and pleasant one.

The nature of prospecting dictates that there will always be some element of tension in every contact. It's just the nature of the beast, a beast you can easily tame with a little courtesy and respect. As a champion salesperson, your success is mind-accomplished before you even begin. Your prospective clients haven't mind-accomplished anything other than using all their fears and worries to build a wall of sales resistance. They're worried.

"What if we lose all our money!"

"What if that salesperson takes all our money!"

"What will we do if we lose all our money!"

Chances are your potential clients are in fact a bit mind-numbed by the experience of actually having to do something with their finances and by the commitment they're mentally debating. To them, you are a stranger who (they hope) has the answers to their questions even though they know they must get answers to their questions.

In their eyes you're someone who could just want to make money off them. Maybe you're trustworthy. Maybe you're not. *"We'll be on our guard just to be safe."* Or, they might agree beforehand that they don't have to make any decisions today, that they'll just listen to what you have to say, getting as much out of you as possible without making any commitment. You know you're a champion, but you have to earn the title every time you step into the ring. Here are three simple steps that help put the skeptics at ease so you can move right into building rapport and trust.

1. <u>Compliment your client.</u> It's easy to find something to compliment if you just pay attention to what you see and hear. Offer a compliment on an article of clothing, a photograph on a wall or desk, a piece of art in the office—anything. Segue into a minute or so of pleasant conversation, which relaxes your potential client, starts the process whereby she begins to like you, and sets the stage for building rapport and trust.

Select your compliment carefully. If their child-beast is yelling at the top of his lungs, tearing your office to pieces and kicking you in the shin, the term "delightful" will not only be (and sound) false, it will mark you as a liar. Of course, you could say, *"Ouch. Quite a little kicker you have there. He'll be a star on the soccer field someday."* Take care of your shins later. Take care of your potential clients now.

Also, make sure that your compliment is sincere. People can spot a phony a mile away and these people are probably within arm's reach of you. Remember they're nervous, on guard and are in a position to easily misunderstand the things you say. Just look hard enough and even in the most challenging situations you can find a legitimate compliment even if it's simply that he or she was punctual in arriving at your office. Use it to break the ice and to propel you into your presentation.

2. <u>Sit facing your clients.</u> That's easy enough to do, especially if they're coming to your office to discuss their needs. If you are at their home, use these words to get to the kitchen or dining room table: *"Mr. & Mrs. Kraft, to do my best for you this evening, it would be best if you two would sit side-by-side at the dining room table. You don't mind, do you?"* As you say these words, gesture toward that room and in the majority of cases, they'll do what you've asked.

When they're across from you, you'll be able to look them in the eyes and you can use your peripheral vision to pick up on any body language clues or Mr.-to-Mrs. eye contact. You'll be in a much better position (literally) to "read" what they're saying.

3. <u>Establish commonalities.</u> Many salespeople feel that this area of finding common ground with people means that you talk, and talk and talk about many different subjects until you find a chord that resonates between you and them.

While it's important to establish that you're "just like them" in some way, don't flounder when trying to establish common ground. Show your prospective clients you're in the same or a similar position in a professional and champion-like manner.

"Bob and Betty, when I'm not helping people acquire the best investments, I'm just like you—a consumer. And just like you I always shop for the best product at the best possible amount. But I'm not an expert on everything I buy. So I look for someone who knows the products and who can help me understand the ins and outs of what I'm shopping for. That's how I make wise decisions. Today, I want to earn your trust in me as an expert on financial strategies. Please feel free to ask me any questions you may have."

Not only does that short speech position you as an expert, it helps put your potential clients at ease and at the same time builds rapport because you have that in common. They know or should be beginning to believe that you are the genuine article and that your sole purpose is to help them find the best investment for their specific needs.

Have No Fear - A Sale Is Near!

Fear creates barriers to genuine communication. It's your job to climb over, crawl under, go around or tear down those barriers. Don't ignore this responsibility. I guarantee that fear is an element in 99.9 percent of all your presentations, whether prospecting or selling. I recommend three steps to overcome fear. (1) Put your prospects at ease. You've just read how to do that. The other steps are (2) ask for information and (3) provide information.

Show your potential clients that you are genuinely interested in them and their specific challenges and in providing a solution that is ideally suited for their needs by asking a lot of questions. Who? What? Where? When? Why? How? Be friendly and courteous, but really research their lives, their needs, budget, goals, likes, dislikes and fears. This friendly inquiry accomplishes a number of goals. It provides you with the necessary information to actually come up with the ideal product or service for their individual needs. It also shows that you're genuinely interested in providing quality service, that you're thorough in your business dealings, and that you're a professional.

Armed with these effective tools you can walk into any selling situation with those butterflies in your stomach flying in formation.

When working with potential clients always put their needs first. That's the way to create business that lasts.

"A purpose is the eternal condition of success."
~ Theodore T. Munger

Chapter 5

Your Questions + Their Answers = A Win/Win Scenario

As a professional in this industry, you know what information you need to have in order to do your job well. To get that information, you need a list of non-threatening questions that will provide those answers. If you don't use proper questioning techniques people can't tell you all you need to know.

Here are a few suggested areas for beginning your questioning. Some people are reluctant to discuss private or financial matters. A great way to begin the process and ease them into it is to use the sincere and straight forward approach. *"Not to be personal, but, in order for me to do a better job for you, I need to ask you for some confidential information."*

- What are your short-term and long-term financial goals?

- List your major debts.

- What type of financial planning have you done?

- How did that work out for you? Why are you satisfied/ dissatisfied?

- Are you renting or do you own your home?

- Accurately describe your current financial situation?

- What investments are you involved in at this time?

- Are you happy with your investments? Why? Why not? Are you interested in alternatives?

- What factors are motivating the current need? A sudden realization that you don't have enough in your retirement program? Unexpected windfall income? Anticipation of major future expenditures? Concern for protecting home and family?

- What would you change about your current financial situation if you could? Why?

- Where do you plan to spend your golden years?

- Do you have any income that you cannot access for a long period of time, such as an account with a penalty for early withdrawal?

- Who is the final decision maker regarding making a change? You alone? You and your spouse together? Is there anyone else you might consult with before making financial decisions?

- What is the best time for making a presentation to offer you a solution to the current situation?

The more you know about these people and their needs and challenges, the better prepared you are to provide the ideal solution to their specific situations. When you ask questions it is essential that you ask, then wait for their answers. Don't grill people like they do on crime television programs. Be patient and truly listen to the answers.

Make notes about them. Never ask questions by rote and never ignore the answers. Information is power, power that will fuel a closing of the sale and a satisfactory win/win scenario for you and your potential client.

Questions Come in Two Basic Forms

During the first stages of the sales process (prospecting, original contact and qualification) champion salespeople let the other person do the talking. The potential client should do about 90 percent of the talking with you contributing only ten percent. Your time to "shine" comes later.

The way you set things up so that your prospective client keeps talking and telling you what you need to know is to ask good questions. There are two types of questions:

- Closed ended questions

- Open ended questions

Closed ended questions can only be answered by a yes or a no. Generally, they are to be avoided because they rarely provide valuable information and they can actually kill the process before it begins. For example, a retail salesperson approaches a customer and asks the closed ended question, *"May I help you?"* The response is often, *"No. I'm just looking."* The sales person is in an awkward position because he or she cannot logically engage the potential client further. "No" automatically cuts you off from proceeding with the sales process. When given a yes/no question by a salesperson, odds are the answer will be "no."

Open ended questions, sometimes called discovery questions, require the other person to give answers that provide more detailed information. *"Are you folks more concerned with asset protection, diversifying an existing portfolio, or in the potential of high returns in a relatively short period of time?"* See? There's no way someone can answer yes or no to that question. The answer must provide some information that you can use to ask additional questions and get even more information.

Top salespeople ask far more than they tell. Ask enough good questions and you'll soon have all the ammo you need to prove that your product is absolutely the best offering for that potential client's specific needs.

Three Guidelines for Asking Questions

Because asking good questions is such an integral part of good selling I've given the matter a lot of study and thought over the years. I've boiled down all that knowledge into three basic guidelines.

Guideline #1. <u>Establish a bond before you attempt to control the process with questions.</u> Establishing rapport is essential because people want to do business with people they like and trust. They'll never get to the trust issue if they don't like you. There's no need (or reason) to attempt to become "best buddies" on the spot, but it is important that your potential client comes to like you very early in the process. This is one of the reasons for the brief chit chat that takes place before the selling begins.

Guideline #2. <u>Encourage "gut reaction" responses.</u> Too often when someone takes a bit to think about their answers, those nasty negative demons creep in and start jamming up the works. Nearly all of your potential clients will second-guess themselves out of doing anything unless you keep the pace of the presentation flowing with information transfer (questions and answers). Keeping up the pace without becoming pushy is an art. Practice, practice, practice until you can keep things moving, moving, moving toward a successful conclusion.

Guideline #3. <u>Make decisions for your potential clients</u>. You have a lot of different products to offer and going through the details of each one would be too time-consuming. The sale could die on the vine before you come to the ideal product for that individual, family or organization in that manner. Asking questions provides the information you need to eliminate the products that don't fit those potential client's needs. For example, if he or she has some credit challenges, you may make the decision to create a "get out of debt" plan rather than an investment plan.

Twelve Goals for Asking Good Questions

Questions must always be asked for a specific purpose. Here are the twelve goals you need to accomplish when questioning a potential client.

1. Use questions to get control of and to maintain control of the selling process.

2. Ask questions to determine the "big picture" of their needs and wants. Continue using questions to narrow down the focus until you have enough information to provide the best solution to their challenge.

3. Ask questions to get a lot of "yes" responses so you create a trend that will get the final "yes" that closes the sale.

4. Ask questions to awaken the other person's emotions so you can direct those emotions toward a desire to own the benefits.

5. Ask questions to determine areas of concern. Often people will voice false areas of concern for any number of reasons. For example, he or she may be using reasons that aren't really logical as a stalling technique. A champion salesperson uses questioning techniques to eliminate false concerns and to determine the legitimate ones. Only then can you address the situation with any hope of success.

Once you know the true concern, you can start demonstrating not only how they can afford your product (you already have the numbers, so you know), but how that investment will potentially produce genuine earnings over time.

6. Ask questions to address areas of concern. This is called the "porcupine" technique. What would you do if someone threw a porcupine in your lap? You'd throw it back. That's exactly what you do in this situation. Answer a question with a question. This approach helps build rapport and tear down barriers to the sale at the same time. Use this technique and you won't get "stuck" in an ineffective presentation.

7. Ask questions to determine the benefits that will trigger the sale. Champions know that people never buy a product or service. They really want the benefits that product or service provides. These people aren't buying stocks or bonds. They're buying a better lifestyle and independent future. They're not buying financial planning. They're buying their retirement dreams and goals. They're not buying long term health care insurance. They're buying peace of mind. Understand that basic fact and make your presentation using those terms.

8. Ask questions to acknowledge a fact. This is an absolute rule in sales: If you state a fact, the potential client can doubt you; if a potential client states that fact, it's true. Use your questioning techniques to help your prospective client to understand and restate those important facts.

When you say it, you're making a sales presentation. When your potential client makes the same statement, it's because they perceive it as fact. Keep in mind that people buy based on emotion and justify their decisions with facts. Continue painting word pictures of that independent retirement, grander lifestyle or whatever motivates your potential client. And then justify those pictures with the facts he or she has just stated.

9. Ask questions to confirm that you can move on to the next step in the sales process.

> *"Have I answered all your questions on this particular matter? Is there anything else you want to know about our company background? Well, then let's take a look at that, shall we?"*

10. Ask questions to involve them in ownership decisions and thoughts about the product you are offering.

> *"Kevin, do you see you and Susan using the return on your investment as a savings plan or perhaps as funds for additional investment?"*

11. Ask questions to help them rationalize the decisions they want to make. Those folks wouldn't be in your office if they didn't already know they need financial services. You just need to reconfirm the wisdom of their decision.

"Jeff, Karen, I have been fortunate to help people in your exact position for many years now. I'm curious, how do you see yourselves enjoying the benefits of going with the Profits, Inc. line of funds?"

12. Ask questions that close the sale.

"As I see it the only major decision we have to make is how quickly to begin having your money make money. Would you prefer to go with a yearly, quarterly or monthly amount?"

These and other straightforward and polite questions allow you to build up a picture of your prospective client's ability to own, the direction you should take your presentation, and whether to politely end the presentation because they cannot afford to own at this time.

I'm afraid that communication through questioning is becoming a lost art. Too many salespeople today jump right into a presentation before knowing what their potential clients' interests are. As we've covered in this chapter, that shouldn't be your challenge. As a sales champion you will study, learn, practice and continue to hone your communication skills. When you master the art of questioning your prospective clients you're well on your way to mastering the art of selling financial services.

"A new rose has blossomed from familiar soil. The ancient ground has yielded the remarkable birth of a wondrous thing. And it is you. Gaze upon it. And be assured that it is real."
~ George Sewell

Chapter 6

Qualification—A Match Made in Heaven?

Your purpose in selling financial services is to discover the true needs of your clients and prospective clients and if their needs match your services then throw everything you've got into providing that product or service. That discovery process is called qualifying. Sure, Mr. and Mrs. Buchanan need an investment plan, but what type of plan best suits their immediate and long-term needs? Does the current economy indicate better results with stocks or bonds? Mutual funds? Do they want to support the local economy by investing in a local industry? If they're the adventurous type, perhaps they'd be interested in oil and gas, precious metals, commodities, or futures. The point is, you can't make a legitimate recommendation until you know their financial status, interests, and their risk level.

Remember that you know significantly more about financial services than the people who come to you for advice and assistance. They may arrive at your office with their minds set on a particular product. For example, they may believe all they need is a relatively low risk mutual fund. *"That's all we want."* At that point they may be right. They may be wrong. You don't know because you don't have sufficient information. That's where your questioning skills come in to play.

After researching your potential client's needs you might discover that they also need more insurance, and some investments in bonds to balance their portfolio. You may learn that they're in debt up to their eyeballs. If you don't offer debt services, you may have absolutely nothing to offer them.

As you continue questioning, gaining information and building rapport, you can begin explaining and providing the full-range of services they'll need. At the right moment you can recommend a program of graduated services that increases as their needs and budget grows. The more you learn about your prospects before you begin selling the more actual selling you will be able to do.

Qualify Your Prospects for Quality Sales

You can't sell what the client doesn't need to own. An effective qualifying process lets you determine early in the process whether or not to continue. Failure to qualify is one of the leading causes of failure to sell. It's really a matter of an efficient use of time. You invest the same amount of time selling an unqualified lead as you do a qualified lead. Yet, the closing rate on selling qualified leads is much greater than that of closing unqualified leads. That's a fact. Qualifying is the step that (1) leads you to legitimate potential clients and (2) allows you to walk away gracefully from those who do not need your product or service.

I'm serious about that gracefully part. You never know how the fortunes of the person you're facing will work out. Don't burn any bridges. Later on you might want to cross them yourself.

How to Determine What Clients Need and Will Accept

I have developed six steps for qualifying potential clients. Learn them and put them to work and you'll quickly see a dramatic spike upwards in your closing ratio. I call the first five steps my N.E.A.D.S formula for qualifying. They help you determine where these people are coming from and where they'd like to go. The sixth step will tell you the amount of money they're willing to commit to get there.

The steps are:

1. Determine what your prospects have now.

2. Determine what they like most about current product or service.

3. Determine what they would like to see altered or improved about their current situation.

4. Determine the decision-maker.

5. Determine if they're in position to move forward with making changes.

6. Determine their investment range.

These steps work wonders when dealing with emotional topics that involve money such as insurance, savings plans, investments, retirement or college fund planning, and other financial services. Here are the six steps that will set you walking in the right direction.

Step #1. The "N" in N.E.A.D.S
Determine What They Have Now

Different people respond in different ways to qualifying. Some will tell you everything you want to know (and more) in considerable detail. They realize you're there to help and the more information you have to work with the better position you'll be in to provide that help. Others may be shy or suspicious, so much so that you'll have to pry the information out of them with a series of polite, but in-depth questions. Money represents security to most people and telling a stranger the details of personal money matters can be quite uncomfortable for them—another reason building trust and rapport early is so important.

Before asking what these folks may consider deeply personal or private questions, say these words: *"Jim, Sarah, not to be personal, but in order for me to do the best job possible for you, I need to ask you for some information you may consider confidential or private."* That sentence will most often soften them up a bit and let them know that it's in their own best interests to answer them. You're not being nosy. You're being professional.

Some of the questions you may need to ask include:

Are they home owners?

What is their current financial situation?

Are they renting?

What are their salaries or income levels?

How much do they have in savings?

How much do they have in investments?

What are their debts?

Are they looking for asset protection or return on investment?

How much insurance do they have, on who and what type?

Do they have an emergency fund? A retirement plan? A college plan?

What do they like/dislike about their current insurance, financial plans, financial status?

These are very personal questions to most people. With the shy and/or suspicious types you'll need to ferret out the information you need, but in a polite and respectful manner. Continue to reinforce the facts that you are an expert in the field and that your only goal is to provide the best possible financial advice for their specific needs. But you need their cooperation in order to provide them with the best service.

Step #2. The "E" in N.E.A.D.S
Determine What They Enjoy Most About Their Current Product or Service

This is essential knowledge. It will play a major role in how you structure the rest of your presentation. For example, if they lack the funds for making realistic investments, have outrageous expectations for returns on their investments, or absolutely refuse to provide the financial information you need, you'll know to wrap things up and move on to a better potential client. Don't think of moving on as a loss, though. It isn't. Because you qualified these people early, you've avoided wasting a lot of time on what will inevitably be a no sale situation. Remember, potential clients are everywhere, so let go of the unprofitable exercises and go after the people you can truly serve.

You've not only eased out of an unprofitable and potentially embarrassing situation, but you've done it in such a courteous manner that the non-client hasn't been offended. In fact, they may know or meet someone with real investment potential and will possibly pass along your name as a straight shooter. Again, never burn any bridges when you qualify. For example, these folks might clean up their acts, get a good credit rating, build up a legitimate investment fund someday and will qualify for the type of financial services you offer. Treat em' right, and they'll most likely come back because of your superior service.

Qualified leads are often pre-sold clients. By asking the right questions you've set up a situation in which they are virtually committed to working with you. It's just a matter of how. They've become involved, partners in a process rather than subjects of a presentation. When you move on to the presentation stage, you're really just reconfirming a mental decision your potential client has already made. Presentation, addressing concerns, closing the sale and getting referrals become natural and easy steps. And you become a hero for solving their financial challenges.

Step #3. The "A" in N.E.A.D.S
Determine What They'd Like to Alter or Improve About Their Current Financial Plan

A champion salesperson builds his or her presentation around what the potential clients like most about the program they currently have in place and how to make it better. Create success by building on success. The simple and straightforward approach is best. *"Louise and Dennis, if you could change anything about your current insurance program, what would that be?"* Then sit back and allow your potential client to tell you how best to turn him or her into a client. Done properly, your clients will tell you exactly what they'll say "yes" to owning.

Step #4. The "D" in N.E.A.D.S
Determine the Decision-Maker

You must determine the decision-maker(s) as early as possible. Why? Because many people like to let you think they're in control but aren't. Dealing with someone who cannot say "yes" to your offer is a waste of time. It's understandable that they'd allow you to think they're empowered to make buying decisions since the program would be in their names, but real, final decision-making power isn't always in the hands of the person you're talking with. Handle this carefully to avoid bruising egos. Someone who can't say "yes" may still have the power to say "no." Even if the potential client lacks that power, someone with a bruised ego could still kill the sale by negatively influencing the decision-maker.

> *"Clark, before we get started outlining a new financial program, is there anyone else who will have a final say in this decision? Is there anyone else I need to visit with?"*

Step #5. The "S" in N.E.A.D.S
Assure Them That the Information They Just
Provided Will Get them Where They Want to Go

The "S" in N.E.A.D.S. stands for the word *"solution."* You must assure each and every potential client that you're a solution-oriented advisor...that your company is, as well. These folks have just bared their financial souls to you. You must once again offer them a statement of trust. Try these words, *"Troy, Amy, as a representative of (name of your company), I have the ability to research and analyze your needs we've been discussing in order to find the right solution."*

Now, you need to get their commitment to finding a solution as well. How do you do this? By asking. *"If we are fortunate enough today to find the right product for your needs at the right level of risk, would you be in a position to proceed?"*

This is a great sentence because it takes a lot of pressure off your prospective client. The magic word "if" indicates that you may or may not find the perfect solution today. That's a real load off the potential client's back because he (or she) suddenly realizes that you're not about to whip out some "cookie cutter" plan or program. You're going to explore possibilities first. There's no commitment in conducting research. Whew! Sometimes you can actually see the tension being released by the potential client. As you make that statement, use your body language to put them further at ease. Use a simple shrug or sit back in your chair.

Once the tension is broken, the other person is more likely to open up and tell the truth about whether he can or can't proceed. *"Well, honestly, Mr. Hopkins, we weren't planning to sign anything today. We just want to get some information to consider."*

Okay, you know they're not intending to make a decision today. And that's all right. You've discovered important information. You know you won't waste valuable time because you'll handle the process differently.

Rather than letting their answer stop your forward motion, simply say, *"I understand. Let me ask, how soon are you planning to make a decision about implementing an effective program for your financial future?"* This question serves two purposes:

1. It asks a direct question. The answer will tell you what you should do next.

2. It subtly tells the potential client that the sooner they have a plan in place, the better.

At this point, they're either going to give you a date down the road that you will take as a commitment from them or they're going to stall which tells you that they're still very afraid to make any commitment with their money and that you have a lot more work to do in your presentation before they'll feel comfortable enough to go ahead.

Step #6. Establish Their Investment Range

Most people you sell to will likely fear making any changes that affect their budgets. They may feel they're already financially strapped. (That may be why they're talking with you.) They won't want to give up what they have now to get what they want for their financial futures. They may truly have no idea of what they can do differently to achieve more. After all that's why the United States alone needs 2 million plus financial advisors in the next few years!

Rather than move forward with a typical plan for someone with their needs, you should first find out how receptive they'll be to a new plan. With your experience, you know there are several routes to financial independence at a wide range of investments. It's wise at this point to find out what range these potential clients will be most comfortable with and most likely to choose. You do that by gently telling them about what other folks have done and letting them tell you what they'll agree to. It's called "the triplicate of choice for money" strategy.

It goes like this: You select three investment ranges for your products and services based on what your clients have just told you. By couching these investments in the proper wording, you won't offend them if you've started too high or make them think you weren't listening if your suggestion is below what they expected.

Start by working with the most economical figure you think would make the most sense for them. Then, come up with another figure that's about 20 – 25% higher. And, another that's about 50% higher. You can adjust these percentages up and down once you master the strategy. The key to the success of the strategy is to deliver the options in this order: 1) 20 - 25% higher than the amount you think they'll go for; 2) 50% higher than the amount you think they'll go for; and then 3) the amount you believe they'll most likely choose.

> *"Carl and Eileen, I've learned over the years that most people at your stage of life who were interested in starting a financial independence program are prepared to invest around $120 per month. A fortunate few can invest between $150 and $200 per month. And then there are those on a limited or fixed budget who, with the high cost of everything today, can't go higher than $100 per month. May I ask, which of these groups do you feel you would fit into most comfortably?"*

It may seem odd, but most people will choose the figure in the middle. I've tested this many times over the years and the result is the same in 60 percent of the cases. At the very least, with those who choose the lowest figure, you're still getting their commitment to a minimum number of dollars they're willing to put toward a financial program. This is an excellent strategy for eliminating the "it costs too much" stall later in your presentation and to provide you with the framework of what products or services to present in the next step.

If you work with a company that utilizes an analysis tool that generates a summary report of where the potential clients are today and shows any shortfalls in accomplishing their goals, you would enter all the pertinent information you gain during this step of the selling cycle into that program. The added bonus of the qualifying strategies covered here is that you get a pretty clear picture of what their acceptance level might be to actions your analysis might deem necessary.

"A wise man will make more opportunities than he finds."
~ Sir Francis Drake

Chapter 7

Before You Present, Think!

With many financial services companies, it's common to present your solution to the potential clients' needs on a second visit. This allows you time to properly analyze their needs and create a customized program to help them achieve their goals. This scenario really takes the pressure off you and allows plenty of time for preparation of your presentation.

As you prepare the solution that is right for each potential client you'll meet with, think beyond their financial needs, to their personal needs as well.

Aging No Longer Means Old

A Greek proverb states, *"The old age of an eagle is better than the youth of a sparrow."* As I write this, a series of television commercials targeted to serving seniors notes that retirement has an entirely new meaning for the current generation of people entering that stage of life. Instead of using images of old people in rocking chairs on a front porch, they show retirees as happy, active and engaged people having fun and being productive.

The *"graying of America"* is a term heard these days and with good reason. The baby boomers aren't babies anymore and seniors are becoming a significant part of the financial services market. And this is not just in America.

Today's 60-plus aged folks who are approaching retirement are using more and more varied financial products than ever before. Instead of getting old in the old homestead, they're out there on skiing vacations, learning new skills, volunteering, traveling the world, and even creating new businesses. Times have changed. You may have to throw away a lot of old ideas about retirement planning and look at our aging population with new eyes.

Still, working with seniors often requires some special consider-ations. First, many seniors experience a loss of hearing and some of your comments will inevitably be misunderstood. Others might not be heard at all or might not be heard correctly. Raising your voice isn't the answer and might even cause an unintended insult. Simply sit closer and make sure you speak slowly and clearly. The other person's responses will guide you as to whether or not to slow down, pick up the pace or speak slightly louder. You can also turn down or turn off any distractions, such as music on the radio, telephones, and sound effects on your computer. If you're in an environment with a lot of extraneous noise, suggest a move to a quieter spot.

Whatever you do and however you do it, do not be condescending. Loss of hearing doesn't mean loss of thinking capacity. Remember, these people have a lot more experience thinking than you do. They may already be pretty savvy with their finances. However, chances are they won't know as much about financial services as you do. Don't discount the fact that they may have been around the block a few times. If you treat them improperly, they'll march out of your office, and find someone else in this business who will treat them as they deserve.

It is important to be prepared to make the same points using different words and phrases. This is particularly important when speaking with seniors who may have trouble making out certain sounds, words or phrases. *"Did he say 'does' or 'doesn't'?"*

Seniors aren't automatically suffering from memory loss or fading minds. Many, if not most of them, will surprise you with the sharpness of their thinking and their brainpower. Still, you'll be explaining terms, conditions, products and concepts they may not be readily familiar with. Break this information down into short and easily understood sentences rather than running a lot of information at them in a single complex sentence. Again, you're not being condescending. You're just breaking a complex subject down into bits and pieces to make it more palatable.

Ask questions until you are positive that you have made and they have understood your key points before making your final recommendation and asking for the sale. Get constant feedback and stay focused. Avoid any topic that doesn't enhance your explanation of the major features of your offering. Keep your presentation simple. Prepare and use colorful, simple visual aids. We'll talk more about that in the next chapter.

Again, use words and phrases that are appropriate to their age group and that are easy to understand in the context of financial services. Improve understanding by using appropriate analogies, metaphors and stories. For example, let's say you want to use a few recording industry terms to illustrate a positive outcome. *"This investment will not only earn you a gold record, it will 'go platinum.'"* That's fine, but instead of using Snoop Dog, Lil' Kim or Brooks and Dunn as examples, you'll probably do better with The Beatles, Elvis Presley or Perry Como.

Give your analogies some thought. Metaphors can be useful, too. *"Owning stocks like these in the current economy is like riding a roller coaster with a lot of frightening ups, downs and bumps along the way. Bonds in this market are more like a gentle ride on a smooth highway in which you know what's around the next bend in the road."* During your qualification stage you'll discover hobbies and interests, so try to use stories related to those interests to help make your point. *"Investing in this product is a lot like investing in your coin collection. The longer you hold on to it, the more valuable it becomes."*

Think before you speak. Use your imagination to make the connection between your analogies, metaphors and stories and the purchase of your financial services. Make that road trip as smooth as possible. Take your time and continue making your points until they understand and see the benefits of your offering. Retired people have more time than employed people. They're willing to invest that time to make the right decision. Be patient. Be under- standing. Hang in there and become their trusted advisor. People buy you more as much as they buy your product. Build rapport. Work hard on gaining their trust so they'll accept your recommendation when you make it – even if you have to work a bit harder to earn that trust.

Your efforts will be worthwhile, especially when you reap the financial and emotional rewards of providing genuine service to your clients. Working closely with the "graying" population is a certain way to keep your own personal financial prospects "in the black."

Boom, Baby!

Rapidly moving into what used to be called old age are the baby boomers, those folks born between 1946 and 1954. At approximately 76 million people in the United States alone, they represent just over a quarter of our population. Retirement is a reality or a soon-to-be reality and they're looking forward to the same perks the seniors in those TV ads enjoy. Fortunately, having been in the work force for decades most of them have savings accounts, homes and other valuable assets, and even investments. Experts estimate that this group has $1 trillion in spending power. They need financial services not only to protect what they have, but to assure them plenty of gold in their golden years.

Although they have assets, they are also using those assets. For example, they may be caring for their children by providing funds for college, a starter home, or some other need. At the same time, they may be supporting or partially supporting aging parents. As retirement becomes a reality, they need the aid and guidance of a knowledgeable and experienced financial services provider.

Baby boomers aren't frightened by the future, but most of them are concerned. They have worked hard to achieve a certain level of financial independence and they'd like to protect or even grow those assets. That's part of your job in providing the services they need. You make sure that the golden future really shines.

Keep in mind that the term "baby boomer" is deceptive. These folks aren't babies by any stretch of the imagination. The post-World War II generation has an unearned reputation for a lack of seriousness. Don't let those old images of Woodstock color your thought processes. Most of the hippies who "tuned in, turned on and dropped out" dropped right back in again, turned on to building better lives, and tuned into the American Dream.

Five Guidelines for Selling Financial Services to Baby Boomers.

1. Don't lecture. Boomers, for the most part, are educated and many of them have embraced the concept of continuing education. You're a provider of services, a counselor, and a partner in helping

them achieve their dreams. Just deliver the facts and provide relevant examples and proof of your claims. They'll get it.

2. <u>Use real life examples to express your concepts.</u> Studies indicate that boomers respond better to this manner of presentation rather than the linear step-one-step-two-step-three approach. They have good imaginations. Engage them.

3. <u>Be careful of the use of the term "experts."</u> Some of those hippies did a lot of protesting and still carry a bit of anti-establishment thinking (even though they're now part of that establishment). Again, use stories and analogies from the real world to make your point.

4. <u>Personalize your presentation.</u> Boomers as a whole are very individualistic. You'll notice that business did not engage in "casual Friday," "flex time" or child care at the work place until after World War II. You cannot use a cookie cutter or "one-size-fits-all approach with this group. They just won't respond. You'll have to earn their business one boomer at a time.

5. <u>You can and should be excited in your presentation, but be prepared to back up that example with facts, figures, benefits, proof and real life experiences to make your points.</u>

As with selling to any group, your goal is to establish long-term relationships. Approach these folks with that in mind and your success ratio will really boom, baby.

Youth Must be Served

A well-known adage states that youth is wasted on the young. Young people don't have the real-world experience to appreciate, grow in, and learn from the real world. But it isn't really wasted time because those are the years when we acquire some of our most important training in life, in work, in family, in everything. That's where another adage comes in to play: *"Youth must be served."* Who is more in need of sound financial advice, products and services than a young individual or family?

The techniques for selling to young people are basically the same as selling to baby boomers and seniors. But this group does have certain needs and challenges that must be addressed.

For example, just like you and I at those ages, young people believe they are invulnerable. They believe nothing bad can happen to them. That's why so many don't have health or life insurance or at least don't recognize having those safety nets as being important. They work out at the gym, jog, dance all Saturday night and just don't see the need for it. Imagine, then the challenge of explaining a long-term health care program to someone who doesn't even see the need for health care insurance today!

That sense of invulnerability is one of your greatest challenges, especially for someone just starting out such as a college graduate getting his or her first job. *"Insurance? Who needs it? Financial planning? Don't see the point. Savings account? On my salary? Besides, I have to save all my money for the weekends."*

More than any other group, young people need guidance. It's not that they're unintelligent. They just don't have much background, base of understanding or training in money matters. Unfortunately, it's just not taught in our schools. That means you'll have to do a lot of explaining and in terms that they grasp. It also means you'll have to prove the importance of deferring some of that weekend fun for wise financial decisions now. *"Now"* is an important term because most of the young people you'll meet are far more concerned with what they're doing Friday and Saturday nights than they are with retirement (insurance, savings plans, investments and you name it).

A young family with a newborn or two may be more concerned with having enough money to by diapers and formula. Saving for a rainy day is important, but they'll feel a need to put that day off for a day, a month a year or more. If their focus is on the baby, your focus will need to be on showing how your programs directly benefit that baby not only today, but throughout his or her life. As with any prospective client, you must learn what is really important to them so you can show how your product or service perfectly matches those needs.

Young families and individuals often feel that they have absolutely no assets. They are often burdened by enormous educational expenses such as school loans, expenses they may have to work for years to pay off. The family may have just moved into a larger apartment or starter home and feels a need to hold on to every penny that comes in. Still, they need some level of financial advice, especially if they are to build a more prosperous future.

This is where you turn the information you gained during the qualifying stage into a sound presentation that just makes sense for them to implement. Most people I have met, including those just starting out or in the lower strata of the economy don't really have just barely enough money to get by on. Someone who can afford to invest even $50 in a Saturday night date or $20 on a day at the lake fishing can afford to invest in some form of protection or plan. Which one depends on their need at the moment—and your ability to make them see the wisdom of taking that step.

Let these young people know that you're not their parent, a lecturer or a drill sergeant. You're someone who wants to become part of their team, an advisor who only wants to help them build that safe, secure and profitable future. Handled properly, me vs. them quickly becomes us working together.

I'm certain you'll encounter other special circumstances as you grow in your financial services career. Perhaps you choose to work within a certain specialty or with clients with similar needs such as doctors and dentists. It's critical that you make solid efforts to truly understand their particular needs and offer them a presentation that is truly customized to those needs. The more they feel that you under-stand them and their situations, the better they'll feel about trusting you as an advisor. As mentioned before trust equals closed sales.

"The people I distrust most are those who want to improve our lives but have only one course of action."
~ Frank Herbert

Chapter 8

Presentation—This is Who I Am, What I've Done and What I Can Do For You

You have two basic goals during the presentation. One is to prove to the prospective client's satisfaction that you are an expert in the field and that you can determine the best solution for his or her financial service needs. Two, you want to show that solution in such a way that your potential client becomes a satisfied client. Part of your task as a professional salesperson is to act as an educator and a lot of this educating takes place in the presentation phase of selling.

As the title of this chapter states, the presentation phase for financial services addresses four basic, yet critical subjects. These are:

- Who we are

- What we've done

- What we'll do for you

- What our recommendation is

If you are to master the art of selling financial services, you must cover these core lessons within your presentation and you must cover them thoroughly. Until your prospective clients fully understand the information in these areas, they will give you verbal and visual cues you need to pay attention to in order to proceed with the sales process. Just as any teacher in any classroom, you must educate so that your students can formulate questions which then allow you to provide even more education – specifically how your offering perfectly matches their specific financial needs.

People Need Three Things from a Presentation

As any good teacher knows, not everything someone needs or thinks he or she needs is necessarily good for them. When it comes to presentations, all legitimate prospective clients have three basic needs and since these are logical and also help you build toward the close, it's important that you cover these essential bases.

1. <u>People need to feel that they are being educated.</u> As a professional this is one of your major goals. It is also important to make sure that these people know that they are being educated. Information and education are effective tools and like any tool they can be abused. A manipulator will withhold or use information to gain an advantage over a prospective client. A champion uses the same tools to discover and meet real needs and more directly involve the potential client in the process. Gaining real knowledge makes them feel good about making decisions and feeling good is critical to ownership.

2. <u>People need to be motivated.</u> Even if you're offering the most exciting and perfect solution, if you don't transmit your own excitement to them, they won't be motivated to own. If you think back, I'm sure you'll agree that your best teachers were the ones who were able to get you excited about the subject at hand. That can be a real challenge because the people you are serving could very well be on

an emotional roller coaster ride. One minute they're totally happy and excited and the next they're worried and depressed. It is your job to keep their spirits up and motivate them to (1) continue with the sales process (which means to continue their education) and (2) see the wisdom of getting involved with your offering.

3. <u>People need to have fun.</u> Again, which teachers made the biggest impact on your education? Those who made learning an exciting and fun adventure top my personal list. I realize that selling financial services is a serious matter and it should be given all due respect. But your clients and potential clients need to enjoy the process. It's perfectly okay to be lighthearted during a presentation, provided it's appropriate and you keep things under control. If presented properly, your clients will enjoy seeing how they can achieve their financial goals. What's more fun than realizing how you can have what you've dreamed of?

Remember, You're Presenting to People

The two most powerful tools at your disposal are your abilities to ask focused questions designed to elicit direct, specific and honest answers. Then, to really listen to those answers. Do not fall into the trap of focusing on your presentation so much that you lose focus on your clients. Too many salespeople ask a question and then never hear the answer because they're already thinking about the next thing they're going to say. This is selling by rote. Actually, it's not selling at all. When you use proper sales techniques, you will know precisely what you need to say during your presentations and when to say it. So, let's examine a championship presentation to see how it works.

Tell 'Em, Tell 'Em and Tell 'Em Again

Champions invest about half as much time in making a presentation or demonstration as average salespeople. Yet they bring in between four and ten times as much business.

Why is there such a large disparity? The answer is simple. Champions stay focused. Top performers qualify people so they know they're working with someone who has a genuine need for the product and can afford to get involved. Champions know their products well, can communicate effectively, and they know how to control the process. Control doesn't mean manipulate. It means to direct, guide or lead people to seeing the answer to their needs themselves. It is just one more proven way to serve the real needs of qualified people effectively and efficiently.

Any elementary school teacher will tell you a simple three-step process for teaching a skill.

1. Tell them what you're going to tell them. This is the introduction of you, your company and your product or service.

2. Tell them. This is your presentation.

3. Tell them what you just told them. This is where you summarize what you've said.

You don't do this because people are unintelligent. Far from it. You use this technique because most financial services clients don't know what you know. What is basic to you may be as mysterious to them as quantum mechanics is to me. Employ this three-step process so your clients can learn, remember and put to use the information you impart.

They will then rationalize the decision to get involved with a program that will help them achieve their goals—preferably your program.

Advertising professionals say that repetition is the key to a successful ad or campaign and this isn't just some ploy to beef up the ad budget. Study after study has shown that people don't realize they've been exposed to an ad until they've seen or heard it six times. That's the reason one of the keys to learning is to read something at least six times. People have to see or hear that same ad many more times for the message to get through. Awareness alone won't get the job done. Learning comes through multiple exposures to the information.

That's why repetition is so important in champion selling. It's not that people aren't intelligent. With a few exceptions I've encountered, they're all a pretty savvy bunch. But they do not know your product. They do not know your company. They do not know you. That's why you have to tell em' what you're going to tell 'em, tell 'em, and tell 'em what you told em. Repetition is how you make sure they internalize the information you provide so they feel comfortable making the decision to accept your offering.

Again, this isn't selling by rote. A champion varies the way he or she makes the same point again and again by using different words and phrases. This is where a lot of salespeople drop the ball and lose focus on what's really important. It's as unfortunate as it is logical. Repetition can become dull. They've heard it and said it a thousand times, so they skip lightly over this necessary step or rush through it. Top performers are always finding new and interesting ways to say the same thing so they continue to enjoy the process throughout their careers. The goal is to have your presentations packed with relevant information, fun and, ultimately, successful.

Give People a Choice

Consider the financial services industry as a big wheel with a lot of spokes. You're the hub, the person at the very center of all the action and the one individual holding it all together. You have a multitude of options for putting together the right combination of products for each client's particular needs. To do this you must know and fully understand your entire product line. You can't truly serve anyone without this background. Armed with product knowledge and information gained from your prospective client through proper questioning techniques you'll be in a position to offer the range of products that meet their individual needs.

Once your prospective client narrows down the number of options during qualification, he's really the one doing all the work at this point. You're just directing the effort. As you provide more specific information on your offerings, your potential client's comments and questions will guide you further toward meeting his or her specific needs.

Everything you do should build toward a successful closing of the sale. As important as the presentation is, it is not the be-all and end-all of selling. Be wary of putting in too much razzle dazzle during a presentation or demonstration. It's important to know where you are, but you must maintain your focus on your ultimate aim.

Use Words Your Potential Client Wants to Hear

Many salespeople fail to serve their clients properly during the presentation stage because they employ overused or tired words and phrases. Each presentation becomes a replay of the one before it and boredom sets in. Spice up your presentation by finding new and exciting ways to say things. Use what I call glamour words. They are words that are commonly know, but uncommonly used. Most often they're adjectives such as exciting, dynamic, timely, and so on. Inserting these words into a dry presentation will liven it up a bit for both you and the potential client.

Let's assume that a young couple has come to you for investment advice. They're employed in good jobs, and they've saved a small amount of money they'd like to turn into a bigger amount of money. Here's how you can address a concern and at the same time employ words and phrases they like to hear.

"Mr. and Mrs. Silvers I realize this investment is an important first step for you."

"It may not seem like a lot of money, but it is to us."

"And that's why I think this investment is perfect for you."

"We were thinking maybe we should wait a year or so."

"Well, that's certainly an option. Do you happen to know how much a Burger King Whopper costs these days?"

"About three bucks. I take my lunch breaks there. Why do you ask?"

"I want to illustrate an important point. Do you know that the original price was only 37 cents?"

"What does that have to do with investing?"

"Everything, Mrs. Silvers, because it has to do with the power of money. Think about this. The sandwich you could have

purchased for only 37 cents now costs almost ten times that. My point is that any investment today will buy more than it will tomorrow, next year or ten years down the road."

"I get it!"

"Exactly. Doesn't it make sense to invest your money now when you can acquire more for your money?"

You see how this works. Their concern provided a perfect way to illustrate the importance of making the purchase right away. It helped that the salesperson illustrated the presentation in words, phrases and images easily understood by the specific client. Again, the Silvers aren't unintelligent. The salesperson just used appropriate techniques to help them see the wisdom of his presentation.

Learn from your presentations. See which words and phrases are a hit and which ones miss. Notice how some work well with single people while others work well with families and so on. Ours is a rich and varied language. Flip through your thesaurus. Play word games or do crossword puzzles. Use words to their best advantage and you'll have a real advantage over your competitors.

Keep Your Presentation Moving

To win we must close the sale and to do that we must provide only the best solution within a limited amount of time. That effort requires efficient preparation on our part because a critical aspect of your product is information, the specific information that will help you close your sale. Now, here's where I'm going to surprise you. That limited amount of time needed to present that information is only 17 minutes.

I have worked with a lot of producers and directors of corporate videos who limit their scripts to no longer than 15 or 20 minutes. Why? Because after that amount of time their viewers' interest begins to decline. It's the same with potential clients. You have a limited amount of time before you automatically start losing your audience's attention. In fact, the more you drone on in a presentation, the less chance you have of closing.

Cut the fat in your presentation. Leave in only the essential and highly valued meat. Then practice, practice, practice until you can provide the necessary information in the allotted time. Know your presentation so well that you look and sound relaxed and confident. Don't panic and try to rush. Believe me, 17 minutes is plenty of time.

Economy with your presentations is a double win. You will have time to visit with more clients during your allotted selling hours each week, while still imparting valuable information. Be prepared, of course, to deliver a longer presentation should the client so desire. Some folks will need you to explain things in more detail. But, there will be others who understand pretty quickly and will appreciate the short-but-sweet version.

The idea is to keep your presentation moving. Keep your potential new clients involved and time will fly. They'll be happily educated and look forward to your next visit.

How do you keep someone involved? There are two ways: mentally and physically. Keep them involved mentally by using your questioning techniques. Show that you are working as a team with them to resolve their challenges and get them the best financial program possible.

Keep them physically involved by providing something to put their hands on. You will have lots of printed matter of interest to your potential clients. Many if not all of it can be printed as handouts which can be used in the presentation and even as take home material. Graphs and charts are excellent ways to compare financial products, show interest rates, timetables, pros and cons, and so on. Early on you may want to present your brochure as proof that you and your company are the best qualified to provide financial services. However, beware that once you hand them something, you've lost their attention to that brochure or piece of paper. They'll want to read it rather than listen to you.

The best way to hand over information is to simply offer it and say *"here"* or *"please look at this"* or some similar phrase. Most folks will automatically reach out and accept whatever you are handing them.

Excuse Interruptions

No matter how hard you try, someone or something will eventually interrupt your presentation. A phone will ring. (Though it shouldn't be yours. Turn it off before going into any meeting with a client.) Your client's phone will ring. Someone will stick his or her head in the door or walk by. A car outside will backfire or an emergency vehicle will pass by on the street. Don't get flustered. Don't panic.

Don't let any interruption throw you. Even if you're screaming inside because you know they were about to say *"yes,"* maintain a calm and professional demeanor on the outside. Accept the distraction, but don't let it distract you from your goal. If the interruption lasts more than a minute or so and actually prevents you from continuing, re-enter the sale by briefly summarizing the presentation thus far. *"Deb and Mike, let's review what we've covered up to this point and see if you have any questions or concerns before we proceed."* Emphasize the benefits of your offering. Interruptions change emotions. When bringing them back into the presentation, bring them back to the emotional level present before the interruption.

Keep It Down to Earth for Heavenly Results

A lot of misguided salespeople enter a presentation as if entering a battle. They talk, talk, and talk, until their poor client surrenders out of fatigue and desperation. Like so many poor leaders throughout history, this type of salesperson may win a battle, but he or she eventually loses the war.

Look at it this way. Do you like and trust someone who pressures you? Would you want to do business with someone so pushy that you can't get in a word edgewise? I do believe that salespeople have to lead their potential clients to seeing the solution presented as a wise choice, but battering them into submission is no way to earn clients, their return business or their referrals.

Potential clients are not the enemy. Each is a unique human being who deserves to be treated as an individual with individual strengths, weaknesses and challenges. Approach every sale as a unique experience and you will find yourself enjoying more successful experiences for your efforts.

Never forget that your client may have had a negative experience with those who practice sales warfare. You may pay a small price in time and energy to overcome challenges put into place by one of those hucksters.

For example, let's say a couple comes to you for help in setting up a financial plan. You're a professional. You have the ideal product, you've been recommended, but you're getting a lot of resistance. What gives? It could be that their previous financial advisor used high-pressure sales techniques to sell his or her product. Your prospective client's defense systems are on high alert before you even meet. The wall was built by someone else, but you have to either break it down brick by brick or climb over it. A low key approach is essential in such situations. Remember, though, that even if they have had a bad past experience, they still agreed to meet with you because they have a need that has gone unfulfilled.

If you're sensing an underlying hesitation, use these words, *"John, Mary, I sense some hesitation coming from you about moving forward. I've encountered something similar with other clients who had a bad experience with another financial advisor. Would you mind telling me what happened in the past to cause you to hesitate acting on something so important to your financial future?"*

Sales techniques are tools, not weapons. Advising, counseling and educating isn't a battle. Keep it low key and allow people to like and trust you so you can address their concerns and provide the best advice for their current situation. The beauty of using what you are learning in these pages is that you can thoroughly guide your presentations without seeming to control the process at all.

Talk to Me

Every occupation has its unique terminology, jargon and slang. If you know a bit of that language you can use it to illustrate your sales points in a way that's familiar and easy to understand.

You don't have to become an expert, just learn enough to enhance your ability to communicate. Sources of information are everywhere. Once you know your prospective client's occupation, hobby or interest you can drop by the local newsstand. Today there are magazines on every conceivable subject. Visit your local library or go online and punch in a few key words. A little bit of information used sincerely will help you to serve your clients well.

I See Your Point (Working With Visual Aids)

Working without visual aids is like walking the high wire blind-folded and without a net. It can be done, but one little slip and you're having a really bad day. It's very hard to recover when you're flailing about and headed for a crash. Visual aids provide ways of illustrating your sales points, offering proof and getting your clients mentally and often emotionally involved in the process.

Your company, parent company or your suppliers probably provide you with a set of standard visual aids: business cards, company brochures, company CD and DVD presentations, Powerpoint slides, charts and graphs, web presentations testimonial letters and so on. Some people in your organization will file most of these tools away and wing it by relying on their own silver tongues and golden voices. Don't be like them.

You will generally find these folks struggling to climb out at the bottom of the success ladder. The top producers become expert at using visual aids for one basic reason. They work! They illustrate complex points. They build confidence. They help close sales.

I think one of the chief reasons low performing salespeople refuse to use visual aids boils down to a misplaced sense of importance also know as their egos. *"All those slides and brochures and things just get in my way. I have the product. I have the service. I have me and that's all I need."* Right. And a high wire walker doesn't need a sense of balance.

Top performers know better. They realize that visual aids are powerful tools when worked properly into a powerful presentation. They get their egos stroked by satisfied clients, closed sales, referrals and repeat business.

When (not if) you hone your presentation down to 17 minutes, you're still going to be spending a lot of "face time" with your potential clients. I don't care how much you look like a young Johnny Depp or those super attractive forensic investigators on the television show *CSI*, it's hard for a potential client to look at just your face for an entire presentation. Visual aids break up the visual monotony, so to speak. (Nothing personal there; you know what I mean.)

Again, winging a presentation is an invitation to fall on your face. Here at Tom Hopkins International we've conducted numerous surveys and studies over the years and two factors relating directly to success are constant.

One, top performers are masters of time management. They know how to get things done well – quickly and professionally.

Two, they focus exclusively on the essential details and little else.

Using visual aids streamlines the process even more. They help you get and stay focused and they keep people involved. They make you more efficient and more effective. Combine them with your ever-increasing professional skills to make the type of presentations that lead directly to the phrase "happily involved" or "satisfied client!"

Organize Your Paperwork so You Can Get to the "Paperwork"

If you've prepared a portfolio, binder or Powerpoint presentation as a visual aid, you must be thoroughly familiar with every page or slide and its location. Your clients will be looking at the material while asking questions and you don't want to be forced into flipping it over to find the answer.

> "What's the pay out on that, Miss?"

> "Uh...here, let me see that...eh...let me just pull that out and see what it says on the back..."

Such lack of knowledge and control is not only impolite, it marks you as an amateur. If necessary, have duplicates for your own reference or write out cues on your notepad before the presentation. I've seen some folks write or tape cues, hints and facts and figures on the back of stand-alone visual aids. Champions are always prepared. They know the answer or have it right at their fingertips.

Some materials to consider if you're creating your own visual aids are a cover sheet with your prospective clients' names on it, a table of contents, company history, charts and graphs to illustrate key points in your presentation about why they should work with you and your company; and testimonial letters or recordings from satisfied clients. These testimonials can be particularly strong when provided by a friend or trusted associate of the potential client who referred them to you.

When using a binder or a presentation folder in which materials can be put in and taken out according to the needs of the meeting, make sure everything you need is in there and in the proper order before every presentation. Each sheet must be accurate and up to date. Flipping for pages that may or may not be there and that may or may not be in the right order shows that you are disorganized. Would you want a disorganized person advising you about your money?

If your qualification of your potential clients has determined the type of specific financial services best suited to their needs, you may target every visual aid to that specific product. If you don't yet know or think the prospects might change their minds during the presentation, have alternatives readily available either in another binder, folder or as an appendix in your original presentation piece. The point is that you have a lot of valuable information at your disposal. Don't dispose of it. Use it to get your client to endorse that even more important paperwork—the agreement.

Feature, Benefit and Proof

It's a basic and essential sales technique to convert product and service features to specific benefits to your client or prospective client. That's not the end of it. You must realize that at that point in his or her mind you are making a claim and nothing more.

You must offer proof of your statements or your perceived claims will remain just that—claims. This isn't a mind game. It is a mental process and one you must use to get the approval on that paperwork. With proof, stated claims become accepted facts, your prospective client can then believe what you're saying and you can move on toward the close.

Proof can be in the form of a favorable article in a newspaper, trade publication or newsletter. It could be a product review or a positive feature or story on your company or industry. Testimonial letters provide the most powerful proof of all because they're praise from people just like the people listening to your presentation.

It's a natural human trait to look for and trust the opinion of the "outside expert" and you can use that trait to your advantage. Have several letters available and be able to point to specific paragraphs or sentences that address specific concerns. For example, if the potential client is "gun shy" about doing business with your company, flip over to the letter praising your company's ethics and professionalism. If the concern is about the product, flip to the long- term satisfied customer.

"There are no secrets to success. It is the result of preparation, hard work and learning from failure."
~ Colin Powell

Chapter 9

Addressing Concerns

Every *"no"* brings you one step closer to *"yes."* Though we may have heard that adage before and agreed with it, it's still hard not to take the *"no's"* personally. Too many people who are new to sales find themselves stopping when they hear an objection. It's almost as if it's a real, physical stumbling block. In fact, *"no"* comes in many forms, most of which we're likely to hear during or immediately following our well-prepared, customized presentation.

We always want to think we have done such a great job in researching and planning our presentation that the decision is a no-brainer for the client. Yet, I'm telling you now that no matter how perfect your solution, you still need to expect to hear objections.

Please realize that making objections to something we want or need is almost an automatic reflex response for most people. No one wants to be thought of as being an easy sale. And, many of us hate to part with our money. When we feel ourselves being moved to do so, the second-guessing part of our mind kicks in and makes us weigh the decision against all sorts of factors that may or may not apply to this purchase. It's a complicated thing.

Our goal in this chapter is to simplify the step of the sales process that comes after presentation. Salespeople who have not been trained by our company will continue to call this step *"handling objections."* Personally, I don't care for the image the word *"handling"* brings to my mind. It's an image of manipulation. So, in keeping with our replacement words from Chapter 4, from now on we're going to call this step in the sales process *"addressing concerns."* A *"concern"* is something that is raised by your potential client and lowered by you through the use of proper selling strategies.

If you believe, as we've said all along, that your products and your exceptional financial advice is truly good for the potential client, it is your obligation to help them realize the benefits of owning it and make the decision to do just that. Going back to our analogy of *"building,"* this step would be the last before the finish work would take place.

The word "concern" is so much less threatening than the word *"objection."* And it legitimizes a potential client's questions without setting up a confrontation that could destroy the relationship.

An *"objection"* is a brick wall springing up in the pathway to a closed sale. A concern is merely a matter to be discussed as you continue walking down that path. Addressed properly, concerns represent the ladder you need to climb your way over that wall. Don't fear them. Learn to love them.

When a prospective client raises an area of concern, he or she is announcing a decision to own. People won't waste their time objecting to something they have no interest in.

You'll Only Need to Address Two Types of Concerns

You will encounter two very different types of concerns:

- Minor concerns

    and

- Major concerns

Minor concerns are not serious issues at all. Usually they're used as a stall, a way to slow down the presentation so the prospective client can gather his or her wits, assimilate information, and follow what you're saying.

Notice this when selling to a husband and wife. One will seem to be following your presentation well and perhaps even agreeing with it. Then the other spouse will start raising all kinds of concerns. They may want you to make a diff e rent recommendation— something with a lower amount. Or this individual might just be confused and need a little time to sort things out. Whatever the cause, it's a stall, not a stopping point. So don't stop.

One of the best ways to determine the importance of a concern is to avoid answering it immediately when it's raised.

> *"Mr. Lembeck, I understand your concern and the answer to your question is part of my presentation. With your permission, I'll address it in a few moments."*

Move on. If the concern isn't raised again, consider it minor and forget about it.

Major concerns can keep your clients from making buying decisions. They need to be addressed carefully, properly and respectfully before you can ask for the final decision. I'll cover the process in detail later in this chapter. First, I want to address another situation you will inevitably face.

A Condition Means "The End"

A condition presents an entirely different situation. It is a logical and valid reason for ending the sales process immediately—politely and professionally. A condition means the death of your sale.

Unlike a concern, you can't go over, under, around or through a condition. For example, if you hear " *We just can't afford this investment"* from someone who has a good job with a reliable income and a solid credit rating, you're facing an area of concern. It's a plea for you to show how the investment he or she wants is affordable and in fact is a good proposition.

If you hear " *Tell me more"* from someone with a bad credit rating, poor health and a history of being fired from a series of low-paying jobs, you're facing a *condition*—unless one of your products involves debt consolidation or counseling services.

In the case of a life insurance product, they may have too many pre-existing conditions to acquire something other than what they already have—at least at a reasonable amount of money. Regardless of their desire for the product, you'd be attempting to sell something they simply can't own or that may not really be good for them. Always remember, first and foremost, the product you're offering must be good for them.

Attempting to work through a condition is a waste of time for both parties. These people need to move on to improve their credit rating, get regular employment, improve their health (if possible) and to build the financial reserves necessary for investment. You need to move on to finding more qualified people and closing more sales.

The Door Is Open

When a concern is raised, consider it an invitation to educate your potential clients further—not as a stop sign. A concern is little more than someone asking for more information. Its use shows genuine interest, not outright sales resistance. Instead of thinking *"oh, no"* you should be thinking *"thank goodness."*

Understand that *"I can't afford it"* is just another way of asking for help finding an investment amount that's comfortable to them.

"I can get a better deal elsewhere" means *"tell me more about the value of your offering."*

"I gotta' go" is just a way of saying *"please give me a reason for sticking around."*

"We need to think about it" is their way of saying *"please give us more to think about."* They may be feeling emotionally moved toward making the decision, but don't have enough information to back it up with logic. They just need help to rationalize the decision.

Handle Fear, Not Objections

After all these years of training, I fail to understand why so many salespeople fear this aspect of championship selling. It's like being afraid of a hammer, a computer, or a cell phone.

By learning effective methods to address concerns instead of giving in to fear, you could easily move on to getting potential clients answering more questions in the affirmative until they agree to approve the paperwork. In this case, it could be that Harvey would be thrilled to say "yes" to a product that's just a little more economical but you'll never know unless you know what to say when he says, "I can't afford it."

Knowledge drives away fear. Invest time studying what some of your more experienced associates do and say when a concern is raised by a potential client. Ask questions. Take notes. Ask more questions and even accompany them on sales calls or presentations to see and hear how they do it.

One way to overcome fear of rejection is to prepare a list of concerns and the manner in which you can address them. We'll cover some of the most common ones here. Study and rehearse them until you can deliver them verbatim and with true sincerity. If you're sincerely interested in what's best for your clients, this won't take long. Remember, most people want and need the services you provide. You just need to help them rationalize the wisdom of their decision to work with you.

If the potential clients raise doubts about a certain aspect of the program you're recommending, it could be that they don't truly understand it yet. Or, they could have known someone who told them that type of investment was a bad thing. You don't know until you ask. Here's how you ask:

> *"Mark, obviously, you have a reason for saying that. Would you mind sharing it with me?"*

This question simply asks them to enlighten you further about what they're thinking. You're asking for clarification before addressing the concern directly—always a wise move. It leads directly into the six-step method for addressing concerns.

Step #1—<u>Hear Them Out</u>

"Them" obviously refers to your clients and potential clients, but it also refers to the major objections themselves. When a potential client voices a concern allow him (or her) to fully express what's on his mind. Make sure he's said all he needs to say before you even think about voicing an answer. This is key because you could easily step on your own toes.

"Tom, I don't think we can afford..."

"Sure you can! Here, look at this chart. It proves that someone in your financial position can easily afford $250 a month for this investment. It's a piece of cake!"

By not allowing the other person to finish the statement, you run the very real danger of selling something that you may not need to be selling. Jumping in like that is pushy and obnoxious. You keep on pushing, never allowing him to break in because that would break your train of thought. Gasping for breath from the effort you keep pounding anyway. That pushy attitude will only push your potential client away.

What if he was just about to say something other than what you were thinking? *"Tom I don't think we can afford $250 a month, but $200 a month is quite within our range."* At that point you could move toward closing a $200 a month program and perhaps work with your potential client to eventually work their way up to that $250 amount.

If you break in when your potential client is voicing a concern, you won't be able to address the concern or close the sale. Listening well requires discipline and practice. The return on that investment is enormous. There's an old phrase, *"Talk is cheap."* Possibly, but when you talk too much, when you talk over your client or prospective client, you can very easily talk yourself right out of a sale. In that case, talk isn't cheap. It's about as expensive as words can get.

Step #2—<u>Feed it back</u>

When someone brings up an area of concern, feed it right back by asking him or her to elaborate on their concern. You sincerely need their feedback. You can't look like you're stalling to figure out an answer to an expressed concern or that you're lost or panicked and need time to regroup.

> *"That's very interesting, Harry. Would you please tell me more about your feelings on that matter?"*

> *Or,*

> *"Obviously, you have a reason for saying that, Sara. Would you mind sharing it with me?"*

It's that simple. When she supplies more information, you politely keep probing with solid questioning techniques until you reach the core of her area of concern. Then you can address that concern appropriately.

Feedback works particularly well when a husband and wife are making the decision together. I've often heard an area of concern, feedback and then before I could answer one of the started addressing the concern, doing my work for me and perhaps, because of their close relationship, doing it better. Feedback is a proven technique, one that feeds back profitable sales in your direction.

Step #3—Question the Area of Concern

By "question" I don't mean for you to act as if you don't believe what's being said. You must be sincere and show that your question is related directly to providing better service. You want to know because you need to know so you can find the ideal solution for their situation.

> *"Mr. and Mrs. Lembeck, I know that you are considering making an important decision. Is the area of concern you have just mentioned critical to arriving at that final decision?"*

Notice that you're not putting anyone down or belittling his or her concerns. You're just seeking information. Notice, too that you didn't blurt out the obvious *"Are you gonna' buy this policy or not!"* That attitude will generally net you the "or not" option. If this point is critical to their decision, you'll have to work with or around it. If it's not critical, you can move on.

By simply asking a polite question to elicit an opinion related to arriving at a final decision you automatically release a lot of pressure from the situation. Tension melts away and your prospective client can think clearly and provide the answer you need to proceed.

Step #4—Answer the Area of Concern

Address all legitimate areas of concern to your potential client's complete satisfaction. They are in the driver's seat, so if they want more information even after you think you've addressed the situation fully, keep on addressing it until they are satisfied. Unless you discover another condition, it is your duty to proceed with your presentation. Don't let the expression of an area of concern throw you. Remember, in doing so they're doing you a favor. They're introducing you to a new friend. Thank them by providing the information they've requested.

> *"That's an excellent question, Mr. Henshaw. One of my clients in a situation almost identical to yours had the same concern. Let me show you a testimonial letter he was kind enough to write about how we helped him."*

Play the "what if" game and mentally make your presentation to your client before you do it in reality. Consider all the areas of concern you expect to arise and how you will address them. When actually making that presentation, listen to every area of concern, address them, but don't dwell on them. Once they're satisfied, move on. Don't kill a sale by over-killing the answer to a question.

Beware of creating areas of concern where they do not exist. Believe me, this happens. Some salespeople focus such intense thought on those negative possibilities that that they actually make them happen. Unaware of what they are doing, they'll provide their potential clients with leading words, phrases and sentences that actually raise the area of concern.

> *"You're not worried about the monthly amount, are you?"*

> *"Well, now that you mention it..."*

Be prepared, but don't be so wrought up in fear that you create the very thing you want to avoid. Again, you want to question the area of concern, but in a way that allows you to proceed with your presentation.

Step #5—Confirm the Answer

Make sure you've really answered the question to the client's satisfaction. Skip this simple step and you guarantee that the concern will pop up again, probably at the worst possible moment. Providing the answer the second time may be more of a challenge because you've already provided the only answer possible. He or she may think you don't know your business.

The way to avoid this challenge is simple. Just ask.

> *"Does that address your concern about the insurance premium (interest rate, payout, penalties, terms and conditions, whatever)?*
>
> *"That clarifies that point, doesn't it?"*
>
> *"Is that the answer you were looking for?"*
>
> *"Do you agree that we've covered this topic fully and have found a good way for you to resolve this situation?"*

A quick and easy way to confirm your answer is to sincerely say, *"Now that settles that, doesn't it?"* While you're speaking nod your head up and down slightly in a "yes" move. Chances are they'll start nodding in agreement and you can move along with your presentation. The bottom line: If you don't fully address the legitimate concern, it will always come back to haunt you.

Step #6—Change Gears

It's remarkably easy for salespeople to fumble around in one stage of the sales process when they should be moving on to the next.

I've seen it thousands of times. Unsure of themselves, they get stuck in "third gear" when they should be shifting into "overdrive." Changing gears is a psychological way of moving from confirming the answer into the next stage of the process. A few carefully chosen words can make a quick and easy transition.

The most effective way to change gears is to combine spoken language with body language. Shift in your chair, change pages in your presentation binder or make some other effective move. Say, "By the way..." Or, you might say, "With that question answered, let's continue."

The combination will allow you to break out of the holding pattern and will help them make that change with you easily, quickly and with a growing expectation of what is to come next—the financial vehicle that will help them achieve their goals.

The single most common concern you'll hear throughout your career is "I want to think it over." Most often this concern masks a money concern. Before you can address the money, you need to get them to admit that it's the real concern keeping them from making the decision to go ahead. Let me provide a shortcut to your education by giving you the words to say when you hear it. Study it carefully and practice it so that it sounds natural when you use it.

> "That's fine, John. Obviously, you wouldn't take your time thinking this over unless you were seriously interested, would you? So, may I assume you will give it very careful consideration? Just to clarify my thinking, what phase of this opportunity is it that you want to think over...(Don't pause after the word 'over.')...is it the quality of the service I'll render? Is it something I've forgotten to cover? Is it the return on your

investment? Seriously, please level with me, could it be the money?"

By the time you hear *"I want to think it over,"* you should have already received their agreement that you offer quality service. You should have covered all the details necessary for a decision to be made including their risk level in regard to returns. That leaves the money, doesn't it?

When you learn that the final concern is the money, don't assume it's a difference between making the investment you suggest and not making any investment at all. Now, it's just a matter of determining what amount they are comfortable with.

"We like your proposal, but we just can't afford it."

Rather than letting that line stop you, be a pro and ask a question.

"I understand, Mike. What amount would you feel comfortable investing in your financial future?"

That question might take you to a different track, but you're still moving in the direction of making a sale—even if it's not the one you originally recommended. Once you gain these folks as clients and they start feeling comfortable with their initial steps into financial planning, they'll come around—if you're doing your job correctly—and do more with you in the future.

Don't let yourself think of stalls or concerns as real conditions until you've tested them by asking more questions. Giving up when you first hear what they think is a condition only leaves the door open to some other salesperson who will do his or her homework, discover that the couple has sufficient funds, and will make the sale.

If there are no conditions and you do not close the sale, the fault is yours and yours alone. More than that, it's a disservice to your client, your organization, and to yourself. When you truly believe in your product and that the person sitting across from you needs it and can afford it, it's your obligation as a professional to help them see it. Then, help them to move forward confidently with a wise decision.

People come to you for financial services because they need and want them. It's your duty to provide those services. Do not let your own nervousness deny those people the readily available benefits you have at hand.

"When dealing with people, let us remember that we are not dealing with creatures of logic. We are dealing with creatures of emotion."
~ Dale Carnegie

Chapter 10

Closing: One Door Never Closes Without Another Opening

Closing isn't the end of the sale. It isn't even the end of the sales process. Closing is the beginning of a long-term relationship.

I define closing as follows: professionally using a person's desire to own the benefits of your product or service, in this case financial services, and then blending your sincere desire to serve in helping them make a decision that is truly good for them.

Closing is perhaps one of the least understood steps in the sales process. Most people think closing is simply asking for the sale.

"If you'll just sign on the dotted line, heh heh." "You, ah, ready to go ahead?"

"Can we wrap this up?" "What do you think?"

"Are you ready to do this today?"

Then there's the infamous, *"You don't want to buy this do you?"*

If you ask for the sale that way, they probably won't want to do business with you. Closing isn't a specific moment in a sale. It's a process. People throughout the free economies of the world have built good jobs, successful careers and business empires on the basic concept of helping people make good choices for themselves. Closing is helping people and isn't that what we're in business to do in the first place?

Going back to the definition of closing, we *professionally* use a person's desire to own the benefits of our product or service and then blend our *sincere desire to serve* them to make a decision that is truly *good for them*. That's powerful thinking for a couple of excellent reasons. One, the definition explains the proper role of the salesperson: serving. You're an advisor and if you've followed the steps I've been giving you up to this point, you're a trusted and liked advisor. Your job is to help. What do you help your clients do? You help them make decisions that are good for them. That's key point number two. You become successful by putting the best interests of your clients first. You fulfill your own needs by providing the means by which they fulfill their needs. Their increasing success creates a need for even more financial services and I think you get the picture.

You may have previously worked for an organization, a department or an office where closing was defined as manipulation. If you haven't heard it before, you will at some point in your career. Please don't buy into this corrupt way of thinking. Make a commitment to be your best and move on to a place of integrity at the first chance you get. A true champion doesn't manipulate anyone. He or she helps, advises, and leads people to make decisions that are good for them.

Manipulators have dollar bills in their eyes and are willing to take just about any steps necessary to close the sale. Clients and potential clients become victims of their greed and ambition.

When and Where To Close the Sale

You close the sale when the time is right wherever you are at the right time. Obviously those conditions vary from person to person and situation to situation, but the more clients you serve the more attuned you'll become to the buying signals that say, *"I'm ready. Close now."* Just like radio waves, they'll broadcast those signals, your salesperson's receiver will pick them up and the situation will just feel right for the close. Trust your instincts. If you've followed the steps in the selling process correctly to this point, the close will come quite naturally.

As you know, you shouldn't change your horse in the middle of a stream, but should your prospective clients transmit change and you pick up on something, anything, that lets you know you're at the right moment, act.

Clients broadcast all kinds of signals.

If they suddenly and unexpectedly slow down the pace of the conversation, they're probably feeling moved to go ahead but are mentally reviewing the facts or their feelings.

If just the opposite happens, they unexpectedly pick up the pace of the conversation, they're probably ready.

If they show some agitation, such as finger drumming or head nodding, combined with a smile or a grin, it's time to close.

When they've been listening intently, but suddenly start asking a lot of questions, you're almost there. When they start using the terms *"my"* or *"our"* know that those are ownership words. They have mentally taken ownership of your product. Now, it's up to you to make it a reality.

"What are the pros and cons of acquiring an annuity now?"

"What is the best type of annuity for me – immediate, deferred, fixed-rate, variable or single premium?"

"Will I be able to move my assets among subaccounts?" "When and how can I withdraw money from my plan?" "How often will the company send me a report?"

When they provide any positive reaction to your answers, they're likely ready to own your offering. Be alert and on the lookout for them.

When in doubt you can always try a test close. A test close, sometimes called a trial close, is simply asking a question that, when answered, shows whether or not your potential client is (1) favorable to your product or service, (2) happy and excited and (3) willing to continue the process. If the response is negative or tentative, you still have some selling to do.

Where do you close? The answer is simple—anywhere. A champion is prepared to close a sale anywhere anytime. Selling can be a challenging and fragile thing. Always be on the watch for the appropriate moment to close. Move too early or too late and you risk losing the sale. The Chinese have a saying, *"The ripe melon falls of itself."* If you have given a championship presentation, the sale will just naturally and practically effortlessly fall into your hands.

Don't think you have to make a big ceremony out of closing. There will be plenty of excitement in the room, office, kitchen, dining room or wherever you find yourself at the right moment. Again, keep it casual. When you reach that right moment don't hesitate a second. Act immediately.

Tom's Tips for Confident Closing

What happens when you're not in your office or a client's home, but you get a definite "I'm ready to buy now" signal? If you're a champion, you let them own. You do your job. You close the sale. If you're not a champion chances are you're completely unprepared. That lack of preparedness could easily cost you the sale. This brings us to the first tip.

1. <u>Always have your closing materials with you.</u> During the delay to get to your office, the conference room, the kitchen table or the living room or wherever you can close, your potential client can develop cold feet. Referring back to that Chinese saying, the melon may fall when it is ripe, but somebody has to be there to pick it up!

Timing is everything. A lot of business is conducted at the club, on the golf course, during lunch or dinner or in any number of non-traditional business locations. Those moments come up more often than you probably think, so start thinking like a Boy Scout and "be prepared."

If you belong to any type of club and already have clients who are also members, you never know when one of them will say, "*Hey, Bob, I have a new grandchild! I'd like to talk to you about setting up a college fund for her. What do you suggest?*"

I'm not suggesting that you lug around a waterproof bag full of paperwork while you're paddling around the community or country club swimming pool. But chances are you have a locker at the facility and one of the shelves inside would make a perfect niche for your materials. Consider any areas where you might store those materials for quick use. You have a car, a briefcase, an overnight bag or suitcase, your office desk and so on. Where could you possibly store closing materials for immediate or at least very quick retrieval?

That's where you want to keep them.

2. <u>Keep those materials neat, clean and up-to-date.</u> You don't want chlorine stains from the pool or grass stains from the links spotting up your paperwork. Make sure all your paperwork is crisp, that you have functioning pens, and anything else you might need, such as a calculator. (Make sure you have spare batteries for that calculator, too.) A sloppy set of materials implies a sloppy sales- person with sloppy work habits. The potential client might still like you, but there's no way he or she will trust you with something as important as his or her financial needs.

Bring out the paperwork before you need it. People often freeze up when a salesperson suddenly brings out an order form or agreement and starts scribbling. The moment of closing is a terrible time to reach for those materials. Have them ready well before the right moment to close arrives. Don't make a big deal out of it. Just ease them out, set them aside, and casually start using them when the time is right. That way there are no breaks in your presentation, just a smooth transition.

3. <u>Use a calculator or your computer software.</u> In our society we often trust machines more than we do our own brains. Figuring calculations on your paperwork can involve math that's more complex than most people use in their daily routines. Even if you're great with pencil and paper and have an excellent mind for math, one mistake, one erasure or cross out can create a lack of confidence. Calculators are inexpensive. If you're careful and know how to use your finger- tips, they're always accurate. A person's learned trust in machines will build his or her trust in you. If your business requires that you do entry

on your computer, demonstrate extra care about accuracy and let the client review the information before you hit the "submit" button.

Close the Sale with Casual Confidence

If you don't have confidence in your offering, your clients and prospective clients won't have it either. Even if you're screaming inside because you're nervous, don't make a big deal out of the close. Just casually start filling out the paperwork. If you've done everything right so far, simply assume the sale. If your timing is on target, chances are they'll nod in agreement. In their minds they've already made the purchase so don't let your personal anxiety get between you and the closing of the sale.

Shut Up!

I know of thousands of sales that have been lost because the salespeople refused to take "yes" for an answer. They missed the "yes" because they refused to shut up. He or she asked a closing question, got a yes response, didn't pick up on it, and then kept babbling on trying to continue closing something that had already been closed. Many times these salespeople have talked themselves right out of perfectly good sales. It happens. Just don't let it happen to you.

Memorize the following words and take them to heart. *"Whenever you ask your final closing question shut up. The first person to speak loses."*

Actually, if the salesperson speaks first everybody loses. The salesperson loses. The organization loses. And the potential client loses because he or she won't make the decision to own the product. By picking up the conversation, you've let them off the hook about making a decision after you asked for it.

Ask your closing question and then shut up. *"John, Mary, with your approval right here, you'll be starting on the road to financial independence."*

You'll undoubtedly start feeling some pressure to end the silence almost immediately. Don't give in. Even if you start perspiring, don't give in. The other person is feeling pressure too. You've asked the closing question and it's time for your client to either decide or ask a question to obtain more information or delay the decision. Be prepared to wait two or three minutes if you have to. If you've done everything right, if you've properly qualified and presented a viable solution, if your timing is right, your potential client should be ready to own. Allow him or her the right to do just that. Waiting patiently is one of the most important and most powerful techniques you can ever learn in sales.

More Ways to Close

You will inevitably encounter folks who will need to have you ask for the final decision more than once. In fact, most sales happen after the fifth closing attempt. So, you need to know more ways to ask for the sale than just one. These "ways" are called closes and I'll give you six for good measure.

In most cases, you'll hear "we aren't ready to go ahead yet." Don't ever end a meeting with a client here. You need to know why they aren't ready and when they will be. It could be that they're just afraid of change—even if it's for the better. People are funny when making decisions about their money. You need to understand that and be prepared to help them make wise ones.

Here's what to say to get them talking—giving you something to grab onto. It could be that they just need more information or another summary on what your proposed program will do for them.

> *"John, Mary, I understand that you're hesitant to start something new. Most people are somewhat resistant to change even when it's a good one they're considering. Please help me understand what you're thinking. Can you elaborate on what's holding you back or when you feel you will be ready to start working toward the financial future we've outlined here today?"*

Most often the hesitation will be about the money. They may just feel the program you've suggested costs too much. When you hear that phrase or any other derivative of it, use the Reduction to the Ridiculous Close.

<u>The Reduction to the Ridiculous Close</u>

This strategy involves converting total or monthly amounts of money into daily amounts.

Step #1: They say, *"It costs too much."*

You need to get an amount of money to work with. Say these words, *"Today most things do. Can you tell me about how much 'too much' you feel it is?"*

They may say, "It's $100 a month more than we had planned on." Now you work just with that amount. It doesn't matter if the total monthly amount you're asking for is $200 or $2,100. It's the $100 that's keeping them from going ahead.

Step #2: Divide amount by 30 days in a month. This breaks down to $3.33 per day.

Step #3: If they both work, break it down further by dividing the $3.33 by 8 hours in a typical working day. That's $.42 per hour.

Step #4: Divide it by the two people you're talking with. That equals $.21 per hour.

Here's how you present it to them:

> "John, Mary, let's look at that $100 for a moment. If you break it down, that amount is only $3.33 per day. You both work full time jobs, so breaking it down further, it reduces to just $.42 per hour or $.21 each per hour. Do you think we should let $.21 per hour stand in the way of the financial future you're envisioning?"

Here you would shut up. It's decision time for them. They either go ahead with the program or will give you another stall. The key to using this particular close is that YOU MUST KNOW YOUR MATH!!!

If they continue to balk at the amount, move on to the next close.

The Oblique Comparison Close

Comparing the daily amount from the Reduction to the Ridiculous close to something the favorable decision-maker would possibly do or give up doing to be involved in the program. "Mary, what comes to your mind that you could do differently in other areas to come up with an additional $3.33 per day?"

If John has a bad coffee habit, she'll zero in on that. Ask John the same question, and you may learn that Mary has been trying to quit smoking or that she subscribes to 15 magazines that go unread. The goal is to get them thinking of something minor or somewhat trivial in their lives that they're currently spending money on that wouldn't really be missed all that much if it's given up. And, emphasize the good that will replace it—moving toward something better in their future.

The Best Things in Life Close

This close is for use with married couples only. You must keep your eyes and ears open when you first make contact with clients in order to be prepared to use this close. When they hesitate, you need to help them see that saying "yes" has worked positively in their lives in the past and will do the same for them on this decision.

> *"Isn't it true, John, that the only time you've ever really benefited from anything in your life has been when you said 'yes' instead of 'no?' You said 'yes' to your marriage (Optional: and I can see how happy you are). You said 'yes' to your job, your home, your car—all the things that I'm sure you enjoy. You see, when you say 'yes' to me, it's not really me you're saying 'yes' to, but all the benefits that we offer. Based on this truth, it just makes sense to say 'yes,' doesn't it?"*

The Fact-Weighing Scale Approach

When your clients want to "think it over" and the "I want to think it over" method for addressing that concern didn't do the trick, or if they tell you they want to "sleep on it" before making a decision, this close is ideal. Use these words:

"In other words, you'd like to weigh the facts."

They'll most likely agree, thinking you'll leave them to themselves to do so. But, no, we're going to help them get it done now. Say these words:

> *"I understand how you feel John, and weighing the facts before making a decision makes a lot of sense. In fact, when I'm in this type of situation, I use a method called the 'Fact-Weighing Scale Approach.' Here's how it works: first, we draw a scale."*

Now, you don't have to worry about being an artist to do this. Just look at my version is here on the page. It's just a visual to get your point across. If you have any artistic fears, think "stick figure."

> *"On the left side of the scale, we pile up, just like small weights, the reasons you feel it makes good sense to go ahead. On the right side of the scale, we pile up the reasons you feel are against it. When we are finished, the decision will be weighed. Let's try it, OK?"*

> *"As far as reasons <u>for</u> the decision, you mentioned that you like the idea of eliminating debt. Mary, you mentioned you'd experience more peace of mind having a larger insurance policy on Brian. Isn't that right?"*

Go for a minimum of six reasons <u>for</u> the decision. Reasons = benefits. You can just draw little triangles, X's or circles to represent the weights.

"Now, what are the weights you feel are against the decision?"

Don't help on the right side! Let them talk. If nothing else, they'll tell you exactly what their fears are about going ahead. When they've finished, say,

> *"Let's see what we've got. On the left side of the scale, we have six heavy reasons why you should go ahead. On the right side, we only have two against. So the answer is rather obvious, isn't it? By the way, I know you will be happy that we took the time to do what you wanted to do, which was to weigh the facts."*

What can they say now? They told you they wanted to weigh the facts. You helped them do just that. They, hopefully, have no other reason to stall the decision.

The "No" Close

Sometimes clients just say "no" and don't give you much of a reason why. Rather than go after the reason why, use these words to help them see what they'll be missing by saying "no."

> *"John, Mary, there are many people like me in the world, representing financial services, and they all have opportunities they're confident are good for you. And they have persuasive reasons for you to invest with them, haven't they? You, of course, can say 'no' to any or all of them, can't you? You see,*

as a professional with (name of your company), my experience has taught me an overwhelming truth.

No one can say 'no' to me. All they can say 'no' to is themselves and their future financial independence. Tell me, how can I accept this kind of 'no?' In fact, if you were me, would you let John and Mary say 'no' to anything so critical to their financial futures?"

These words imply that they'll be losing by saying "no" instead of what they'll gain by saying "yes" as with the "Best Things in Life Close." With some experience, you'll get to where you know which strategy will work best with each type of potential client.

The Similar Situation Close

This is where you relate an example of someone else who was in the same or similar position your new client is in. The other parties may have been hesitant but made the decision to go ahead and today are so happy they did.

For example, following a military mission into hostile territory or even a trip into space, it's standard operating procedure for the participants to undergo a debriefing session during which they review the mission. It's a great way to learn from your success and from your closing attempts that were unsuccessful.

Every champion salesperson I know holds a personal debriefing session after every sale. What did I do right? How can I use the story of these clients to make another sale? What brilliant strategy did I use to regain control? What do I want to repeat?

If you did not end up closing the sale, ask yourself, *"What did I do right?"* Think about all of the things you did correctly right up until the moment this meeting became a non-sale. You need to feel good about all of that before analyzing what you would do differently if you had a second chance. Then, don't dwell on the lost sale. Instead review it in your mind as a learning experience. Then, ask yourself, *"If I had it to do all over again, what would I do or say differently that might change the outcome?"*

Powerful words, phrases and sentences often come to us unexpectedly in a presentation. Like manna from Heaven, they drop in on us and provide sustenance. Write down these little jewels. Analyze them and the effect they had on your potential clients. If warranted, use them again and again. These debriefing sessions will become one of your most important and most powerful learning tools.

Review leads to reward.

Closing Thoughts on Closing

Ultimately you are there to use your skills, abilities and knowledge to help your clients and prospective clients make decisions that are good for them. You are an advisor, trusted counselor, and a leader. Once you understand their needs, fears and desires, it's your obligation to lead them to make the right decision. Then, you will be, in the very best sense of the word, a true financial services champion.

"There will come a time when you believe everything is finished. That will be the beginning."
~ Louis L'amour

Chapter 11

Getting Your Next Client from Your Last Client

We've reached the final step on the right side of the selling pyramid from Chapter 1. You've come a long way from finding your clients *here, there and everywhere.* Now that you've closed the sale with your new clients, you have an excellent source of new business right in front of you. Look no farther at this point in time.

Getting referrals is essential to growing your business. Sadly, a lot of good salespeople lose good sales opportunities because they never ask for referrals. I believe there are two basic reasons for these failures.

One, they forget to ask. They get caught up in the excitement and emotions of closing a sale and forget to accomplish this basic and simple task. That's easy to understand, but hard to believe. A good salesperson will have presentation materials at their fingertips at all times—even if their fingertips can only access the Internet or their email via mobile phone. He or she will make notes during every presentation. How hard is it to have a sticky note with the word "referrals" on it stuck to one of your presentation materials or slapped onto your notebook? That's not a very challenging task at all, is it? Consider making "Ask for Referrals" the copy on the main screen of your mobile phone or PDA.

The second major reason for not getting referrals is that people are afraid to ask. Some salespeople believe that such a request is impolite or pushy. The client might resent the request and cause a loss of business or at least negative "word of mouth" advertising in the community. That's just not true. Have you ever heard a friend, neighbor or relative of yours say, *"Can you believe the nerve of my insurance agent? She just asked if we could help her find more business. What kind of business person does that?"* A smart one, that's who.

That insurance agent wouldn't have gotten the outraged person's business in the first place if she didn't get him to like her, trust her, listen to her and take her advice and counsel. When people like you, trust you and listen to you, they'll want to help you, too. Once they're satisfied clients, they'll be happy to tell the world about what great service they have, what a good person they worked with, and so on. If you ask for referrals at the proper time and in the proper way, you will get referrals. People will be happy to provide names and even provide personal introductions especially if you set the stage properly.

Tell 'Em What You're Going to Ask 'Em

One of the best ways to overcome any concern a client or potential client may have about making referrals is to let him or her know at the beginning of your presentation that you will be asking for referrals at the end.

> *"John and Mary, you haven't seen a tremendous amount of television advertising about our company, have you? (Only say this if it's true!) The reason we don't spend millions of dollars in advertising is because we have chosen to build our business on word-of-mouth recommendations. When we've satisfied your financial service needs, done the job and you're totally thrilled with what our company has done for you, would*

you have any challenges with me asking for an introduction to a few other people I might serve?"

If you work with a company that does invest "millions of dollars in advertising," adjust your opening to something more appropriate. *"John, just like your business, our business grows primarily through referrals."* Or, adjust the dollar figure and the media reference to your specific market... *"hundreds of dollars in our weekly paper... thousands of dollars on the radio..."* These short sentences will go a long way to getting the referrals you want when you want them.

Use Tom's Simple, Yet Powerful Steps to Getting Referrals

Step #1. Help your clients think of specific people they know who might need your product.

Step #2. Write down the names of the referrals.

Step #3. Qualify the referrals.

Step #4. Ask for contact information.

Step #5. If your client doesn't have the contact information handy, ask for their help in finding it.

Step #6. Ask your client to call and introduce you to the referrals.

Step #7. If your client is nervous or refuses to make the call, ask if you can use his or her name when you contact the referral.

That's not exactly rocket science, is it? But if you apply those seven, simple steps you will see your referrals "blast off" to new heights of success. Here's a detailed look at each step.

<u>Step #1. Help Your Clients Think of Specific People They Know</u>

Who might need your product? A champion salesperson doesn't just say, *"Jim, you don't know anybody else who might want to invest in high-yield stocks, do you?"* Why? Because champions know that nine times out of ten the response will be, *"Not right offhand, but let me think about it and I'll get back to you."* And nine times out of ten they'll never get back to you. If you call they'll probably say they thought about it, but couldn't come up with any names.

That lack of success is your fault because you failed to control yourself and the situation. After the close, clients are excited and their peace of mind is high. However, in 60 days or less, they may forget your name if you don't do your job correctly. Providing you with a referral or two is the last thing on their minds—unless you put it there.

The key to success with referrals is to lead your client into visualizing real people not just names in an address book or in an electronic file. They need to see mental pictures of the possible referrals. As a champion salesperson you're an expert at painting word pictures. Put that incredible skill to work.

Give your clients focus. By turning your request into specific groups of people in your clients' minds, you lead them to focus on the real needs of real people they know and will contact in the immediate future. Who knows where those thoughts will lead? You will, but only if you ask.

"Mary, you mentioned that you were discussing your concerns about your financial situation with someone at work. Who was that?"

"John, during our conversation you referred to not being taught much about managing your money while growing up. You said you have several siblings, didn't you?"

Step #2. Write Down the Names of the Referrals

Mental notes are dangerous. They disappear almost at the instant they're made.

*"Oh, heck! Was that Joe Doe or Joe Dough? Is it J-O-E or J-O?
Male or female?"* And so it goes. Write down the name immediately.
Carry 3x5 index cards, use an electronic note pad, PDA, or fast-forward to a blank area on your hand-held recorder and record the information. If you don't record it in some fashion right then and there, consider it lost.

Get the correct spelling. Is it D-O-E or D-O-U-G-H? Is Joe a full first name or is it short for Joseph or Josephine? Be sure to note any difficult pronunciation. Spell out the name phonetically. *"Joe pronounces his last name, Dough, as 'dug.'"* This will be important when you make actual voice contact with the referral. Imagine the impression the salesperson from the previous example would have made had he called Mr. RaMIRez Mr. RAMirez? People are sensitive about such things and they should be. A simple mistake can create enormous and complex challenges before you even get the opportunity to tell them why you contacted them in the first place. This fact is all the more unfortunate because it is so easily avoided. Just ask the question.

Step #3. Qualify the Referrals

Remember, champions invest their time only on qualified leads, people and organizations most likely to purchase their offerings. You'll do extensive qualifying when you talk with them at a later time, but start qualifying your referrals the moment you get them. *"Mary, what brought Sally to mind when I asked about someone who might have a need for my services?"* You don't want to impose on your client by conducting an in-depth interview (unless he or she is okay with that), but you do want some basic information.

You can use this important information in "breaking the ice" when you meet with that person. The initial conversation will be easier and flow more naturally. You'll start building rapport right away because you have shown such interest in addressing her challenges. After you've acquired this basic information, move on to the next step.

Step #4. Ask for Contact Information

This is an important step. Do not skip it. Why? Imagine the challenge when you're back in your office and flip open your phone book to see that Joe Doe is listed fifteen times, Joe Dough seven times, and Jo Dieux three. Well, you know there's a potential client in there somewhere so you invest a day or two trying to contact each one. That loss of valuable time is totally avoidable. *"Do you have his address and phone number or his e-mail address?"*

It's possible that your client will even have the business card of the referral and will pass it on to you. If he wants to hang onto the card, just step over to the copy machine and make a copy. Business cards can provide a wealth of other information.

For example, they may contain a nickname: Joe "Skippy" Doe. They may have a web address and a corporate slogan or motto that can give you insight into the referred person's thinking.

Step #5. If Your Client Doesn't Have the Addresses

Have immediate access to either a print or online phone directory. Sometimes your client will have the information and sometimes he or she will not. Don't let that cause you to skip this step. Get out the phone book or get online so you can get the address and phone number immediately. I can't over-emphasize how important this simple step is to your future sales effort. If you don't get the contact information you may never make the contact.

If the referral is a business owner, flip over to the yellow pages to see if there's an ad with additional information. If so, make a copy or make a note to copy the ad back at your office. There might even be a map or a listing of major cross streets to help you find the location.

Step #6. Ask Your Client to Call and Introduce You to the Referrals

This step is so simple yet I'm amazed so few people ever ask the question. Most beginning salespeople are afraid to take this step and that's why so many of them remain slow-starters for so long. I know otherwise very good salespeople who actually refuse to make this basic request. I have to believe it's only because they don't truly comprehend the power of it.

A personal introduction is one of the most powerful referral techniques you can employ. In essence, it's a personal endorsement of you, your product and your organization. It can be really powerful when your client makes the call while you're with them and he or she is full of excitement over their new program.

This technique is now even more powerful since the Do Not Call Registry was put in place. If the referral's name is on that list, as a salesperson, you cannot originate the call. But your client can. The introduction can be made and permission to contact them directly can be granted.

Some clients will be hesitant about making a call. They may fear breaching a friend or associate's privacy. They may be uncomfortable being involved in the process for fear that you'll not take good care of their friend or associate and they'll look bad. They may have personal reasons, such as shyness or a fear of obligation. If you sense this, back off immediately and move on to the final step.

Step #7. If Your Client is Nervous or Refuses to Make the Call, Ask If You Can Use His or Her Name When You Contact the Referral

Don't bother questioning why a client won't make an introduction. Move on. Ask permission to use the client's name when you contact the referral. Most people don't have a challenge with this at all. It's a fact that the client purchased the product from you and, more important, giving permission relieves him or her from any responsibility for your further actions with the referral.

Always hand out three business cards to each of your clients and ask them to give them to anyone they know who might be in the market for financial services.

"Mr. Ramirez, I so appreciate the opportunity to have helped you create a sound investment portfolio. I'd like to make the offer to provide the same level of advice and service to anyone you come in contact with who might have need for financial services. May I give you three of my cards to keep handy for

when the subject of financial services does come up between you and your friends or business associates down the road?"

When you make your next contact with your client, within seven to ten days, ask how things are going. Ask if there are any challenges or questions you can handle. During this conversation ask if the client has given your card to anyone. If the answer is yes, ask for that person's contact information. If the answer is no, thank them anyway and ask again that they give them to anyone they know or meet who is looking for financial advice. You may again need to trigger their thought process by mentioning the parents of the kids' soccer buddies or the other members of the ham radio operators group they belong to.

Your request for referrals must be casual and natural. It cannot sound "canned." How do you prepare so your presentation doesn't look rehearsed? You rehearse over and over again. Practice, practice and practice until the request flows as easy as a conversation with an old friend. Keep practicing and in a shorter span of time than you think, it will become an easy and automatic element of your presentation.

Follow Up for Even More Referral Business

Follow up is much more than sending a thank you note, dropping a line now and then, or sending a friendly e-mail that you're ready to serve them whenever the need arises. Good service flows out of good record keeping. The more information you acquire and maintain about your clients, the more opportunities you will have to make contact. You don't have to compile FBI-style dossiers. You just need to know a lot of relevant information about your clients. Who are their children? What are their hobbies and interests? Do they have pets? Where do they work? What's going on in their lives? Compile enough information so you can logically make a friendly contact at least six times a year.

Regular follow-up achieves a number of important goals. One, you stay in contact so if their situation changes, you are already foremost in their minds. You also enhance your professionalism in their eyes. Without intruding you're always there for them. Additionally, regular contact makes your clients feel important—as they certainly are. Eventually you almost become a member of the family, something like a distant, but well-liked cousin. And, thirdly, with every follow up contact you have the opportunity to ask for more referrals. People meet new people all the time. Kelly and Sandy Carpenter may have just joined a new golf league. They're meeting all sorts of new people who could have a need for your services.

All follow up contacts should be sincere and caring. This technique worked so well for me that by my third year in business my business was 98 percent referrals. Most of my follow up involved hand-written notes. Today, you have the benefit of being able to automate your follow-up contacts.

Your contacts shouldn't always be about selling financial services; you want to determine their wants and needs. At some point nearly all of your clients will face changes in their lives that require changes in their financial plans. For example, let's assume that some time ago you provided Mr. and Mrs. Barbella with a long- term strategy for assuring financial independence in retirement. One day you pop in for a visit and learn that rather late in life they are unexpectedly expecting. In about nine months there'll be a little bouncing baby Barbella in the house. This is certainly a major change. They are still in a somewhat delighted state of shock and are obviously, to you, in need of a new evaluation of their financial needs.

For example, you could inquire as to whether they've yet considered increasing the amount of life insurance they own. Since a lot of their planned spending will now be spent on other matters, you could ask if they've thought about redirecting some of those monies into a college fund. The lives of your existing clients are in a constant state of change. Some changes, like baby Barbella, are more dramatic than others. But their needs for financial advice and services change with them. Often they don't realize the new needs until an experienced professional brings them up. You can't bring them up unless you discover them. A simple call or visit to determine current wants and needs is the way you do it.

The people, and their business, are out there. If you open your mind (and your files) the opportunities for finding and contacting them are endless.

Three Strikes and You're In!

I'm referring to "strike" as a hit, as in to strike gold or to strike it rich. There are three proven ways to make a "hit" with your clients just by following up on your previous calls.

<u>Follow up by telephone.</u> This is the fastest and easiest method. Just pick up the phone and make the call. I know, that's easier said than done. Mr.Ramirez, being a busy man, may have an executive secretary or an assistant who sees it as his or her duty to block phone calls to the boss. Even if you get through you may only get voice mail. That's not the end of the game. Prepare a short presentation that highlights your respect for your client, your professionalism and your desire to continue serving his or her financial needs.

Too many salespeople are caught unprepared. They don't preplan the message they'll leave if they don't reach a live person. They get flustered, frightened and then they blow an opportunity to make a good impression. To avoid this trap, follow this format: (1) state that you're sorry you missed him/her, (2) state a purpose, such as serving (or reviewing) his financial service needs, (3) say you'll be calling again, and (4) if he'd like to speak to you right away you'll be available by phone and then give a date and a window of opportunity.

> "Mr. Ramirez, this is Tom Hopkins with Acme-Finance-Plus, 555-5555. I'm sorry I missed you. In reviewing my notes, I see that your daughter is just about ready to go off to college. Major changes in life such as this often require a new look at your financial plan. We should arrange a time to review your financial needs from here forward. I'll phone back or if you'd like to speak right away I'll be in the office today from one till five and tomorrow from ten till four. Again, thanks and make it a great day! Tom Hopkins. 555-5555."

<u>Follow up by direct mail.</u> It's easy to drop the latest informational brochure in the mail. It's easy, but it's not very personal and may not necessarily be targeted to the client's current need. How could it be? You haven't spoken so you don't know your client's current need. This is follow up, but it's not very effective follow up. When you use direct mail, use it creatively. Send an article, a clipping, a feature story, even a cartoon that you know your client will find interesting. Include a short, hand-written note. You can also develop a newsletter filled with information of interest to your clients. If you cover a lot of subjects, circle the one best suited for Mr. Ramirez.

Please note that when I say "mail," I include e-mail.

<u>Follow up in person.</u> I know that in this day of cell phones, e- mail and text messaging the thought of a face-to-face follow up meeting might be considered a waste of time. If you're prepared and organized, an occasional "pop by" visit to your clients can be a very profitable use of your time. By dropping in you may not be able to see your client. Mr. Ramirez may be away from his office or in a meeting. That

really doesn't matter. Leave your card so he'll know you called. He'll be impressed by your thoughtfulness and professionalism. After all, considering all the electronic communication gadgets available, who else is making the effort of dropping by these days? You'll be different and in selling, different is good. It helps you to be remembered.

If you haven't been "referring yourself" to your old clients, start doing so right now. Think about these words of Sir Winston Churchill. "I like things to happen; and if they don't happen, I like to make them happen." Getting new business from old clients is one of the best ways to make things happen.

"The sale merely consummates the courtship. Then the marriage begins. How good the marriage is depends on how well the relationship is managed by the seller."
~ Theodore Levitt

Chapter 12

Attitude Makes or Breaks You, Your Career and Your Future

Here we are at the foundation of our selling pyramid. You might wonder why it's the last chapter in the book. I understand better than most how important your attitude is. If you don't have a good attitude, all the selling skills in the world won't lead you to success. However, after 30-plus years of training I also know that people who turn to my training want the "how-to" first. They want to know where to find new business, how to make good first impressions and close sales. They don't come to me for attitude material.

In fact, we don't advertise our company as a provider of motivational material. However, most of my students become highly motivated after they have learned the art and science of selling. You see, what I do is to help eliminate those feelings of being in over your head, of being a less-than-competent salesperson, by teaching you what to do and how to do it. Now, that's motivation!

We have heard the phrase "attitude is everything" so many times over the years that for some it has become a meaningless platitude right up there with "a winner never quits and a quitter never wins." These phrases are mocked in sales meetings throughout the country—except by the champions. Why? Because attitude really is everything. A positive attitude is an essential element in the foundation of your success in mastering the art of selling financial services. Without a good attitude there is no art.

It's not something you're born with, inherit or buy from the business shelf of the local bookstore. Attitude is something you create within yourself and it's something you must create every day.

When I wake up in the morning I like to listen to upbeat content whether it's the spoken word or music. I do this while I'm working out or getting ready for the day. I do so because the first things you do in the morning shape your entire day. I like to arrive at work all pepped up, excited and full of enthusiasm for taking on the challenges of the day. How do you think I'd feel if the only early morning input I got was the latest news about the fighting going on in the world, the famine over here, the tornado or tsunami over there, or the terrible state of the world? If I did that, some days I'd have a tough time getting up on stage and giving my best performance to my students. Worse than that, my negative attitude would infect the people around me. No sir! Life is too short, too exciting, too productive and too much fun to fall into that trap.

How does one develop and maintain that positive attitude? Let's look at some of the challenges that create a negative attitude so we can understand and overcome them.

Crisis Management

When I say adopt and maintain a positive attitude I am not encouraging you to become a "Pollyanna" or look at the world through rose colored glasses. I mean be realistic, but optimistic. No matter who you are, where you are, your status or condition in the world, you will continually face crises in your life. One of the best motivational speakers of all time was Og Mandino who said, *"If you are a human being and alive, you are either going into, in, or coming out of a crisis most of the time."* Look at the math in that. Two out of three stages can be considered negative! We have to make a concerted effort to stay positive.

How can someone have a positive attitude knowing that he or she is in or heading into a crisis? As a champion you know you can't change the nature of things, but you can change how you react to the challenges nature brings. With the right attitude you can manage any crisis, reduce its severity, reduce the amount of time you invest on it, and you can learn and profit from the experience. The challenge isn't in the crisis itself; it's in how you handle it.

Wrong Way

"Bobby, we've been thinking this over since our last meeting and, well, I just don't think we can afford the financial plan you've outlined."

"Are you sure, Mr. Hall?" "Yeah, pretty sure."

"Okay, well, I'll check back with you in a few months."

"Sure. Maybe we'll be ready by then."

Right Way

"Bobby, we've been thinking this over since our last meeting and, well, I just don't think we can afford the financial plan you've outlined."

"Mr. Hall, I can see that this is a real concern for you. Would you mind telling me a bit about your change of mind?"

"Well, we were just running the numbers last night, and I'm just not sure we can afford everything you recommend."

"I can appreciate your feelings, Mr. Hall. So, let's take another look at those numbers just to make sure we're both on the same page. All right?"

"Okay."

The crisis is a client who has developed a case of buyer's remorse, a common malady. Bobby #1 allows himself to be defeated without even a struggle to overcome that challenge. Bobby

#2 knows he has the cure for the malady and, more than that, his positive attitude will not allow him to allow his client to make a bad decision. After "running the numbers" again and seeing how those numbers relate to his needs, Mr. Hall will see the wisdom of making the purchase and how he can handle it.

Or, if he still has cold feet, Bobby will break the financial plan into pieces that are more palatable to Mr. Hall. Maybe he's just the kind of person who needs to start small, testing his comfort level with Bobby and the products recommended. Bobby will likely get Mr. Hall happily involved in the entire program when he's more comfortable with making those decisions and with Bobby's level of expertise in the field.

As a salesperson working in the financial arena and the emotional frenzies that can be associated with earning, saving and investing money, you'll probably face more challenges than most working folks. You willingly (often unknowingly) knock on the door, step in, and walk right up to crisis on a daily basis. You have to face rejection constantly. You'll endure crisis situations that might send the average business person to the corner tavern, to the bottle of pills, or to the rubber room. Challenge is just part of the job, but it's a part of the job you can handle and even profit from. A little preparation and mental training will see you creating and maintaining a strong, positive attitude regardless of the crisis at hand.

The first thing to do is to shift your thinking. Notice how in the previous paragraphs I shifted emphasis from "crisis" to "challenge." You can do the same thing.

Don't endanger your career by ignoring the reality of the many and varied stressors that come with a career in financial services and the fact that they can cause enormous challenges virtually every day. Stand up for yourself and your career and overcome these five challenges that I refer to as stressors.

Stressor #1 – Fear. When you're dominated by fear you expect misfortune that never really happens. Hmm...that sounds a lot like "worry," doesn't it? Fear makes us so emotionally uncomfortable that we avoid doing the very things necessary to insure our success. For example, a lot of beginners are terrified at making personal contact with members of the public. If they don't overcome that challenge, fear will overcome all their efforts and they'll never be top performers. You can't sell all the time by phone, letter or e-mail. You have to get out there and shake hands.

Again, shift your thinking about fear. Instead of seeing it as some giant unconquerable beast, think of it this way: FEAR is nothing more than False Evidence Appearing Real. If you're afraid of shaking hands, that's just false evidence. The reality is most people will want to shake your hand. You provide a valuable service and one that is constantly in demand. Why wouldn't they want to meet you with open arms?

The best way to overcome fear is to charge right into it—straight on and with all the strength you have. Face it. Overcome it and then add its power to your arsenal of abilities. My mentor, J. Douglas Edwards gave me these words about overcoming fears and they've made all the difference in my life: *"Do what you fear most, and you control fear."*

When you challenge and overcome a fear, you'll be amazed at the strength you gain from it. It's added to your existing strengths and makes you even stronger overall. If you're afraid of shaking hands, go out and start shaking hands with people you already know. If the thought of cold calling terrifies you, put down this book and make one right now. Stalling the necessary won't get it done, will it?

If public speaking scares the heck out of you, join Toastmasters or take a Dale Carnegie course where you'll be taught to develop your speaking skills. Make shaking hands, calling on strangers, speaking in public or whatever else you fear a habit and that habit will be the weapon that drives out fear.

Stressor #2 – Rejection. Rejection is part of the job. As sales-people we know we'll hear "no" many, many times more than we'll ever hear "yes." Those are just the rules of the game. The key to overcoming the stress of rejection is to realize that you personally are not being rejected. Maybe you made contact after they've already bought from someone else. Perhaps they're not qualified for your offering right now. They may be experiencing a life-changing event and can't make big decisions at the moment. The timing may have been way off. Whatever the cause of the rejection, it's not you. Never take rejection personally. Shake it off and move on to the next potential client.

Stressor #3 – Disappointment. If you're selling financial services you are in the disappointment business. The reason is basic human nature—people don't always do what they say they'll do or even what is in their best interest. They fib. They forget. They drop the ball. They disappoint.

Realize and accept two facts of life in selling financial services: (1) you're in a position to earn incredible amounts of money while experiencing personal satisfaction and (2) part of the price you pay for that success is disappointment in others. It comes as part of the package. Once you realize that fact of business life, you'll realize that the best thing for you to do is to put that disappointment aside, let it go and then get on about your business.

Stressor #4 – Guilt. Success in selling financial services, and I mean real success, requires a lot of sacrifice. You may have to work long hours at first, often including nights and weekends. This can put some strain on family life. It's easy to miss out on family functions, meal times, weekend getaways, sports activities and so on. It's also extremely easy to go on a personal "guilt trip" because of those sacrifices.

Provided you live a balanced life overall, the sacrifices may well be worth the effort for a defined period of time. After all, your long hours are dedicated to providing a better, more secure and happier lifestyle for your family. Keep your head clear and you will find balance. You will find time. And you will succeed without guilt.

Watch out for underachievers who will try to use a "guilt trip" to bring down your success level. Losers and also-rans are very uncomfortable around champions. Real achievers are a constant reminder of their own lack of ambition and effort. They'll try to build themselves up by bringing you down. Don't buy into that twisted thinking. Surround yourself with other champions so you can energize each other. When it comes to success, they'll be your biggest boosters. Champions cheer when other champions achieve a victory. And why not? We're all on the same team!

The only time you should feel guilty is when you allow your sense of guilt to overcome your drive for success.

Stressor #5 – Procrastination. Someone once joked to me *"Let's form a Procrastinators Club."* I said, *"Yeah, let's work on that next week."* It took him about three seconds to get it. Consider the wisdom of the ancient Roman philosopher Seneca, *"While we are postponing, life speeds by."* Or, to paraphrase Benjamin Franklin, it's putting off till tomorrow what you know you should be doing today. The definition I like to use is this: *Procrastination is living yesterday, avoiding today and thus ruining tomorrow.* It can be as deadly to a career as a fatal disease is to a body.

Here's how you can cure procrastination or any other bad habit for that matter. Commit yourself to "doing it now" for 21 days and then stick to that commitment. Science has proven that we require 21 days to eliminate a bad habit or develop a good one. I don't know what the magic is in 21. Perhaps it's three times "lucky seven." Who knows, but I do know that 21 is the magic number.

Repeat your commitment verbally when you wake up in the morning, right before you go to bed at night, and often throughout the day. I believe you will be amazed at how effective this simple procedure can be. But start right now. Don't procrastinate!

Trash the Trash

In the context of this book, I define trash as anything preventing you from achieving tremendous success selling financial services— anything holding you back. A bad habit, such as smoking, too much drinking, not enough physical exercise, a lack of spiritual or intellectual development, putting off making calls or reading up on new products or anything else that holds you back from the success you can and should achieve. Here's a short list of the types of trash you should send immediately to the trash heap.

Trash dwelling on your failures. We all fail. We are all going to fail again and again. So what? It's part of the process. Focus on learning from the experience. We live in only one time—the NOW. The present is all we have to work with. Yesterday's gone. Anyway, the past is past and tomorrow has not yet arrived. Focus your efforts on succeeding in the here and now.

Trash needing everyone's approval. Receiving everyone's approval is truly an impossible goal. When you exceed your quarterly goals and have served yourself and your company magnificently you will make the higher ups very happy. But at the same time you will make some of your co-workers and competitors very unhappy. They'll be jealous of your success and embarrassed at their own failures and they'll react by offering their disapproval.

The only way some people think they can look good is by making someone else look bad. Real achievers have these big targets painted on their backs. If you ignore the negative efforts of negative people, then the barbs and bullets they shoot your way will bounce off as you continue merrily on your way.

Trash listening to underachievers. No matter where you are you will always encounter someone who will tell you that you can't do something or that something won't work. That something is usually a proper step in the achievement of your own success.

Underachievers have a more serious effect on beginners who haven't learned the ropes and who haven't learned how to discern the difference between achievement and the appearance of achievement. Still, underachievers love to give advice and they're very clever about how they deliver it. That's another reason to limit any time you spend with underachievers so you can invest the majority of your time with champions. Choose your associates carefully. The price tag (and I do mean price, not investment) is just too costly.

Trash getting angry. Anger is a powerful enemy. It can cost you sales, ruin relationships, end a career and destroy a business or a family. The really disastrous thing about anger is that it can become so consuming. Getting even, getting payback, and making someone else suffer becomes an overwhelming goal. It devours everything including your time, your thoughts, your emotions, your energy and your health.

It's just not worth it. Turn all that negative energy building up inside you toward a positive outcome. It's a philosophy very close to one I've adopted: *Don't get mad, turn them around.* If I allow myself to be consumed by anger I am allowing myself to be controlled by another person's actions or opinions. He, she or they automatically win because I'm the one being manipulated. I'm immediately off the success track.

What do I mean by turn them around? When clients are angry or appear to be angry, most of the time they just need to blow off a little steam. I'm serious. They may be railing against you over the return on investment or the interest rate or any number of matters when they're really angry at a spouse, one of their own clients, or the bad driver who cut them off on the Interstate.

The key is to avoid fighting fire with fire. Fight it with water, calm, cool water. Be friendly and open. State that you're glad they're airing their situation with you. Let them know you sincerely want to hear their concerns. Take it easy and don't give into the temptation to "fire back."

Listen and show you're listening with appropriate body language. Say "yes" and "I hear you" and "I understand" and encourage them to keep talking. In most cases they'll burn out all their anger within a couple of minutes. There will be no more steam in the engine. I've had a number of such incidents in which the accuser actually apologized. Handled properly, such situations can actually strengthen the relationship.

Control your anger and you can control the situation.

<u>Trash expecting fairness in life.</u> Let me tell you a little secret. There's no such thing as fairness. One day your sales will be on fire and the next they may be as cold as ice. You'll have good months and you'll have bad months, but that has everything to do with business and life cycles and nothing to do with fairness. There will be times in your life when you face challenges that seem unfair. Do what you can. Change what you can. And deal with the rest as best you can.

Too many times people use the word unfair to cover their own failures. They failed to make their quota of prospecting calls, but that's not the reason for a drop in sales—unfairness is. They didn't get the promotion, but it's not their fault—it's just not fair. Sales are down, but it's not their fault—unfairness is the cause.

The excuse becomes a "comfort zone" where the salesperson can continue to fail or underachieve without feeling guilty. After all, it's not his or her fault. Life's just unfair. Watch out for this self- induced trap. Don't get bogged down in such feelings. They can be almost as crippling and as dangerous as anger.

What do you do when all the garbage cans in the house are full? You take out the garbage. Throw it out. Get rid of it. Take some time within the next day or so to discover what kind of trash you've allowed to accumulate in your mental house. Examine it. Bag it. And take it out to the curb!

Use the Law of Attraction to Attract Sales

The Law of Attraction has been known and practiced for thousands and thousands of years. More recently, a DVD/Book called *"The Secret"* by Rhonda Byrne has brought it worldwide attention. The bottom line of the book, the movie and all the take-offs from it is that whatever you think becomes your reality.

This is the *"secret"* that all the world's greatest achievers have known and used throughout history. I first learned this from Earl Nightingale in the 1960s. I found it hard to believe but tried it anyway. I constantly thought about doing so well in my sales career that I'd be winning awards and soon found myself winning all kinds of sales awards. If you have any doubts, I challenge you to pick out three to five high achievers you admire and then read their biographies. If you boil down the essence of their achievement it will be *"I thought I could do it, and I did it."*

You can, and should, apply the law of attraction to everything in your life, especially your efforts to sell financial services.

Here are four affirmations that will engage the Law of Attraction. I want you to read and believe every morning. Take them to heart.

1.   *My attitude every day will determine my success in the future. Today, I will walk, talk, act, and believe like the person I wish to become.*

2.   *I deserve success and will do what successful people do. I will refuse to allow negative people to fill my mind with negativity.*

3. *Most of the arguments I have are with myself, so when I get down, I will use the G.O.Y.A. (Get Off Your Anatomy) formula for guaranteed success.*

4. *Today, I will win. Why? I'll tell you why – because I have faith, courage, and enthusiasm.*

The Law of Attraction works—provided you believe it works. That is the key. In fact belief is the key to everything. Have total faith in your ability to become a champion in the financial services industry. That faith plus your focused actions will inevitably turn your dreams into a solid, undeniable, wonderful reality. William James expressed this beautifully when he wrote, *"a fact (may) not come at all unless a preliminary faith exists in its coming…"*

Believe in your company and your industry. Believe in your product. And believe in yourself as I believe in you.

By choosing this wonderful career selling financial services, you're in the people business. More than that, you're protecting assets, building the futures for individuals and families, and helping businesses thrive. You're one of the key players in the American economy and the American dream. You make a direct and powerful impact on the lives and fortunes of thousands of individuals, families, companies and organizations. Be proud of that. I am.

"The greatest revolution of our generation is the discovery that human beings, by changing the inner attitudes of their minds, can change the outer aspects of their lives."
~ William James

Additional Resources

There is a wealth of information available online instantly and for free. Check out the web sites of associations for your industry. Here are a few to get you started.

ACLI - American Council of Life Insurers at
http://www.acli.com

AFS – Americans for Financial Security at
http://www.afswebsite.org

AIA – American Insurance Association at
http://www.aiadc.org

AIDA – International Association for Insurance Law in the US
at http://www.aidaus.org

AIE – Alliance for Investor Education at
http://www.investoreducation.org

AIMS – American Insurance Marketing and Sales Society at
http://www.cpia.com

ASEC – American Savings Education Society at
http://www.chosetosave.org

BISA – Bank Insurance and Securities Association at
http:///www.bisa.org

CFA INSTITUTE at
http://www.cfainstitute.org

CIAB – Council of Insurance Agents and Brokers at
http://www.ciab.com

FINRA - Financial Industry Regulatory Agency at
http://finra.org

FMA – Financial Management Association at
http://www.fma.org

GAMA – GAMA International at
http://www.gamaweb.com

IIABA - Independent Insurance Agents and Brokers of
America at http://www.iiaba.net

IIS – International Insurance Society at
http://www.iisonline.org

IMCA – Investment Management Consultants Association at
http://www.imca.org

MFEA – Mutual Fund Education Alliance at
http://www.mfea.com

NAAIM – National Association of Active Investment
Managers at http://www.naaim.org

NAIFA – National Association of Insurance and Financial
Advisors at http://www.naifa.org

NASD – National Association of Security Dealers at
http://www.investopedia.com

RIMS – Risk and Insurance Management Society at
http://www.rims.org

Many of the larger organizations also have statewide affiliates that can provide invaluable information on local markets, conditions and trends such as the Independent Insurance Agents of Arkansas (and Broward County and Delaware and Georgia and so on.)

Learn Even More Financial Services Selling Strategies!

The Art of Selling Financial Services

Recorded live at a seminar for your industry!

These 4 CDs are packed with skills to help you find and close more business. After listening to these 4 CDs, you will know how to:

- Set and achieve your goals for success
- Find new business - here, there and everywhere
- Gain the trust of potential clients by what you say and how you say it
- Get potential clients talking—telling you what they want to own
- Close more business
- Do what the million dollar income-earners are doing

This program includes 4 audio CDs and a 5th CD with printed matter in PDF format.

RETAIL VALUE - $145.00

ORDER YOURS TODAY AT

www.tomhopkins.com

Why You Should Visit:
www.tomhopkins.com

▽   *To Subscribe to Tom Hopkins' FREE, Monthly E-Newsletter and Receive Additional Training Tips, Articles and Closes*

▽   *To Learn About the Latest Sales Training Educational Products Developed by Tom Hopkins*

▽   *To Find Out When Tom Hopkins Will Be Presenting a Live Training Seminar in Your Area*

▽   *To Download Free Training Aids*

▽   *To Register for Tom Hopkins Three-Day Boot Camp Sales Mastery Seminar for Total Immersion in His Powerful Selling Strategies*

▽   *To Hire Tom Hopkins for a Customized Sales Training Presentation for Your Sales*

CPSIA information can be obtained
at www.ICGtesting.com
Printed in the USA
BVOW06s1514160717
489439BV00017B/292/P